MW00678799

Hill-Pehle Publishing

www.lulu.com/hillpehle

2012

Rattlesnake Revolution by Dean Allen

ISBN 978-1-4276-9500-0

www.RattlesnakeRevolution.com

Published in conjunction with LULU Publishing
and Echo House Publishing.
Cover design by Danniel Hill

Rattlesnake Revolution

The Tea Party Strikes!

by

Dean Allen

Dedication:

This book is respectfully dedicated to
my fellow veterans, and to every
soldier, sailor, airman, marine,
law enforcement officer, or firefighter,
who has worn, or is wearing,
the uniform of our country.

These are the only folks,
other than the Lord Jesus,
who ever offered to die for you!

Other Books by Dean Allen:

Non Fiction

Tax Revolt © 1978

Offshore Asset Protection © 1993

Freedom 2000 © 1998

Homeland Volunteers © 2009

The Battle Plan [Co-authored with Bill Rhodes] © 2010

Coming Soon:

Non-Fiction

Rattlesnake Revolution – The WORKBOOK

American Exceptionalism

Fiction

Ghost Town

DISCLAIMER

Although the author and publisher have made every effort to ensure the information in this book was correct at press time, the author and publisher do not assume, and hereby disclaim, any liability to any party for any loss, damage, or disruption caused by errors or omissions, whether such errors or omissions result from negligence, accident, or any other cause. Everything in this book is presented for information, education, or entertainment. The author and the publisher are not engaged in the practice of any licensed profession. You are advised to seek the services of an attorney or accountant if you require professional services.

Table of Contents

ACKNOWLEDGEMENTS

The English poet and clergyman John Donne (1572-1631) is remembered for saying *no man is an island.* We conservatives are a fiercely independent lot, and writers must, of necessity have quite a bit of ego in order to spend an inordinate portion of our lives writing our thoughts for posterity. All said, if indeed this tome makes any substantial contribution to American political thought and opinion, it will be in no small part because your not so humble author can indeed stand upon the shoulders of giants.

I will forgo the litany of intellectual and literary figures from history who have influenced the course of my life and contributed to the maturity of my prose. I would, however, be remiss if I failed to acknowledge at least a few living Americans who have had a substantial impact on my ability to research and write this book.

Foremost among these would be a mentor and muse who is also a dear friend. Dr. Christina Jeffrey has inspired and encouraged me in countless ways and my efforts would be far less successful without her guidance, her example, and even the occasional admonition to consider carefully the words I choose, and the path I tread.

Hugh Cort, M.D., allowed me to travel the country during a presidential campaign and enabled me to interact with conservative activists from the Iowa Presidential Straw Poll, to the cold snows of New Hampshire, and particularly all over my adopted home state of South Carolina.

Many others have given me advice, insight, encouragement and friendship during the years I have been observing and participating in the tea party movement. I am grateful for the assistance of Bill Rhodes, Dan Herren, Chris Lawton, Dr. Buddy Witherspoon, Calvin Cowen, Dr. Jeff Lynch, and Magda Aguila.

My friends Michael Faw, and Roger Buckner, encouraged me to put my insights into written form and share them with America. They also provided me extensive logistical support and critical analysis as this book was written. My publishers David Hill and his beautiful wife Melissa P. Hill made the process of publishing and marketing understandable. They have also been very involved in the tea party movement in Texas and were an invaluable resource as well as genuine friends.

I am very grateful to Rick Driver at radio station WAIM in Anderson, South Carolina, for his friendship, encouragement, advice, insight, and information. I am particularly grateful for his assistance in creation of the audio version of this book; and, needless to say for frequently interviewing me on the air in a major media market in my adopted home state.

Fellow Cajun, Dr. Marvin Hebert & his charming wife Benita in Houston, Texas, have guided my life and career for many decades with an abundant supply of love, prayers, information, and at times much needed and appreciated logistical support for my mission in life.

Robert Williams in North Carolina, Rick Knox in West Virginia, Robert Smith and Steve Beren, both in Washington state, Dr. William Carter here in South Carolina, Grady Warren and Pastor Terry Jones, both in Florida, are just a few of the many folks who have kept me in touch with the social revolution sweeping across America as well as offering insights into the political races around the country; all are true friends and mentors. I am deeply grateful to Congresswoman Michele Bachmann for her role as Chairman of the Tea Party Caucus in the US Congress now has 66 members, including Reps. Mick Mulvaney, Ron Wilson, and Tim Scott, from here in South Carolina. I also appreciate the time Michele Bachmann has given from her busy schedule, to me and several of my close friends to explain just why this movement, and this election are so crucial to the restoration of our nation.

In the final analysis all the advice and understanding of my friends, business associates, political allies, and family made it possible for me to research and write - and improved the quality of my writing; but, any opinions expressed, and any errors - if such there are – rest solely with Dean Allen alone.

INTRODUCTION

Through this book I use the grammatically correct lower case *tea party* when the term is used as an adjective to describe something; and, I capitalize *Tea Party*, when it is a used as a noun to describe a specific *Tea Party* organization, i.e. the tea party movement; and, Tea Party Express, Tea Party Patriots or Tea Party Nation. There are also some organizations that use the acronym TEA for *"Taxed Enough Already"* and maintain the correct usage is therefore *TEA party*.

If you are reading a book about the tea party movement because you are a lefty hoping I will trash the tea parties; this is not the book for you. If you are lazy, or particularly if you are a pessimist, convinced things will just get worse no matter what we do, put this book down, you are not going to like it either. If, by chance, you are reading this because you want to start, or join, a local tea party organization, and get it organized to begin *fixing* problems in our country, keep reading. This is your how-to manual.

One of the salient features of the tea party movement is the absolute fact the movement is disorganized, unorganized, amateurish, rife with factions, local and parochial in nature. This is neither a criticism, nor is it an endorsement of those conditions, merely an objective observation.

Somewhere north of 90% of the leaders and participants in the tea party movement like it disorganized, most tea partiers see the fractured lack of structure, heavily dependent on local people and conditions, as some sort of virtue. They take great pride in not being part of the establishment they distrust, or, in some cases, actually despise.

There are advantages and disadvantages to being intentionally disorganized. One of the greatest fears of each local group and the local leader; is being taken over by some other leader, organization, or movement will change or dilute the focus of the existing body. In the parlance of the tea party, they have a real paranoia of being *hijacked* as a movement. As a long time movement conservative who is very sympathetic to the goals of constitutionally limited government and free enterprise; my challenge is how to offer assistance to the movement, without being seen as a threat to its autonomy.

Clearly, any assistance to the tea party must not attempt to take over either the movement, or any of its constituent parts. My goal is not to compete with the work being done by tea parties around the country. It is rather to give them the tools and information to become more professional and effective as they continue to work for the same goals they already have. People new to the conservative movement, of which the tea party movement is the latest addition, often ask why it is not possible to unite all the small, fractured, independent, organizations and groups supporting freedom, and opposing government waste and excesses, into a larger structure would have more power by virtue of greater size and efficiency?

The answer to this question is in the way conservatives think. We are first and foremost individuals rather than members of some collective group or organization. We have a fear of large powerful organizations, rather than seeking to become one ourselves. This book, and the related website, offer a tool may be useful to local groups in becoming more effective. Those who find my words useful are welcome to any benefits. There is no plan to take over tea parties, compete with them, or take on the useless task of trying to unite them into some grand conglomeration seeking power. Tea parties don't work way, and they never will.

We will discuss what works, and what does not work, in the realm of influencing public policy and changing American culture. There are tools will make any tea party, more effective and we look at some of these in **Chapter Eight**.

It is very helpful to view the tea party movement in the context of other social, religious, and especially political, movements have shaped and changed the American cultural and political landscape. This continent was settled largely by English speaking people who were motivated by two desires, they wanted to have the economic prosperity of free enterprise; and the ability to worship our Creator according to the (predominantly Christian) dictates of their conscience, and without interference from any governments.

The first major social and political movement on the North American continent was in fact a tea party! Specifically, what later came to be known as the *Boston Tea Party* of December 16, 1773. This is dealt with in detail in **Chapter One**. That tea party led to a violent revolution and the adoption of our current constitution.

Other social and political movements in America have had varying degrees of success. There have been numerous socio-political movements changed our culture in significant ways. These include race/slavery, prohibition, the War Between the States, labor, women's suffrage, prohibition, anti-war protests, so called civil rights, and pro-life, just to mention a few prominent examples resulting in legislation.

Almost all such movements go through a life cycle consists of a *crisis or problem*, sparking *mass protests*, turning into *organizations*, gaining *political power* and influence, used to cause *legislative change*; and, finally in many cases, *outliving their usefulness* to become a thorn to society. The last two thirds of this book discuss these stages in the development of socio-political movements, contrasting those developments with of the tea party movement to date. Without this historical perspective and understanding of the life cycle of political movements, you will be less effective as a local leader of your own tea party organization.

When it is possible to make clear observations, based upon undisputed facts, I have a tendency to speak plainly and describe things as I see them. This is the antithesis of so called political correctness. One of the things I learned a long time ago, from watching my wife and all her lady friends, she loves to *talk* about problems. I, on the other hand, am less inclined to *talk* about a problem and more likely to just *fix* it! I tell my wife all the time; if you want to talk endlessly about your problems, talk to your lady friends. Do not tell me about a problem unless you actually want it fixed - 's what I do, fix things.

When I get together with one of my buddies, as I did earlier this week, we are usually going to fix something - in this case it was the radios in his airplane. Those radios were obsolete. No point in talking endlessly about them, we flew to the man who could replace them and got the necessary information about alternatives and made a decision how to fix the problem.

My wife pushes the wrong button on one of the remote controls and screws up our TV reception on a regular basis. She will say, *"Honey, the TV is messing up again."* We all know inanimate objects have volition, and regularly vex wives just for spite. My wife and I both know my job in this house is to *fix* her *"little technical problems."*

The purpose of this book is to show you exactly how to *fix* the technical problems with American politics and government. We are not here to *talk* about them. Suppose you have been to several of the best physicians in the country, and all are unanimous in a diagnosis of cancer. Would you be looking for still more diagnosis? Would you want the next doctor you visit to suggest additional x-rays, CAT Scans, blood tests, and biopsies? Of course not! Once the diagnosis is clear, no matter how unwanted; you shift from diagnosis to treatment. You want an Oncologist to tell you all about chemotherapy, radiation, surgery, nutrition, and the mental and spiritual components of an aggressive course of treatment leading to a full recovery.

The world is full of books, writers, radio and TV personalities, journalists, and particularly elected officials, who are pessimists able to describe the problems of this country in great, depressing, detail. We already know Mr. Obama is a racist who hates white people, is a committed Marxist, and he was raised by a daddy and step-daddy that were each devout Moslems.

This book has not been written to *talk* about problems, but to *fix* them! This is not more pessimistic diagnosis. We already know things are screwed up, we need not debate the matter, nor should we wallow in it. You and I are here to understand how the imbalance in our body politic led to the spontaneous generation of the tea party movement. We are also here to provide guidance to this movement and begin the process, working together, of *fixing* problems in this country.

How in the world, you may ask, is the tea party movement going to *fix* anything? After all, it is splintered in twelve dozen directions and is totally disorganized. Guess what? The tea party movement is going in a twelve dozen directions because there are twelve dozen places where failure to follow the constitution has caused an imbalance in the American body politic. New recruits to any army are always undisciplined, and devoid of any conception of strategy and tactics, much less, customs & courtesies. That does not mean they will not become fine soldiers. They just need a crusty old Sergeant Major to whip them into fighting shape. See yourself in role.

One of the criticisms leveled against the tea party movement is it does not have any clear plan or program. Most participants know nothing about *vision quests*, and if they understand *creeds*, or *mission statements*, they do not have either. The tea party, according to its critics, is purely reactionary. It only came into being because of fear of, or hatred for; Barack Obama. The tea party, its' critics say; exists only to harass Mr. Obama, his plethora of Czars, his regime, the left leaning media, and the Democrat Party.

Remember I am in the habit of speaking plainly rather than sugar coating things. All those accusations are completely true. The tea party movement is largely a reaction to the far left policies, and radical social changes, were pushed by George W. Bush, and which are being pushed now by Mr. Obama and his cronies. It is particularly a reaction to the destructive levels of waste, spending, and debt, associated with the policies and plans Obama euphemistically calls *Democratic Socialism*.

I was in Washington, D.C., on the National Mall, September 12, 2009 for the largest political protest in the history of the world. **Chapter Three** of this book discusses it in more detail. Almost two million of us assembled to exercise our rights to petition for redress of grievances. I remember seeing a homemade sign, on a sheet of poster paper, fairly summed up the reactionary nature of our movement. The hand-lettered slogan read: "*Obamacare, shove it down our throat in 2009 and we will shove it up your ass in 2010!*" 's a fairly accurate summary of what the Democrats did in 2009 when they controlled both houses of Congress; and how the American people responded in the 2010 elections.

The next criticism leveled against the tea party? It was just a flash-in-the-pan and was not going to be a relevant factor in the long run. Critics hoped, more than believed, the tea party would be a fad like *Hula Hoops* or the *Rubik's Cube*; a fad which would soon disappear. Three years into this movement, it is evident to all; the tea party movement is here to stay! The movement fundamentally realigned the US Congress in 2010! The GOP would not have won a majority in Congress without the influence, energy, and enthusiasm, of the tea parties.

The Republican Party abandoned its own principles and platform by 2006 and wallowed like an elephant stuck in quicksand. The Bible says *"Where there is no vision the people perish..."* Proverbs: 29:18. Republicans abandoned the wisdom of leaders like Ronald Reagan. It was Reagan who reminded us, *government is not the solution, government is the problem*. Republicans were content to merely point out they were not the Democrats.

The American people were fed up with *socialism lite* from the Republicans. We stopped sending money to the RNC, we stopped working for nominal Republican congressional candidates who embraced fiscal irresponsibility as moderation, and immorality as diversity. Republicans lost seats in congress in both 2006 and in 2008, and without those seats, we lost the Speaker of the House and all the power and influence went with the position.

In 2008, Republicans lost the presidency to a known racist with no executive experience. We lost to an agitator whose political allies, and closest advisors, were actual communists who planted bombs - bombs killed policemen!

The election of Barack Obama had an effect on this nation not unlike the shock and anger America felt after the Japs bombed Pearl Harbor. In both cases, the enemies of freedom had awakened a sleeping giant. Ordinary Americans - a cross section of the middle class - poured into the street to demand a return to sanity. They carried hand-lettered posters. They were disorganized, they were confused about what they wanted to accomplish or how to do it. They had no prominent leaders, and few eloquent spokesmen.

This *tea party* mob was angry at congress as an institution for abandoning all sense of fiscal responsibility. They were angry with the main street media for being very slow to report the causes of the now evident economic meltdown. They were angry with the Republican Party for not more forcefully opposing *Democratic Socialism* and providing America with any meaningful alternative.

Above all; they were angry with themselves! They were angry because they had never gotten involved, leaving civic affairs to

20

others. They were angry they had never educated themselves about what made the economy tick, or how the political process worked.

With all its confusion, disorder, inexperience, and anger, this unorganized mob, calling itself tea parties, poured into courthouse squares all over America. The angry, mob, had no legal counsel, no public relations flacks, no membership cards, and no formal organization of any description. In spite of all the anger drama and mass confusion surrounding them, it is precisely this movement, now saving America from moral and economic collapse. When movement conservatives were outnumbered, surrounded, and down to their final bullet, at the very last minute, the Cavalry arrived in the form of tea parties.

That much is history. This is not primarily a history book, though we will look at our roots from time to time in order to understand American exceptionalism. The world is not going to end on December 21st 2012 in spite of inscriptions on ancient Mayan ruins, or what the hippies in Haight-Ashbury think. We are going to fight a battle in November of 2012 will be nothing short of the American Armageddon. This book is a **How To Win Manual**.

Others have dwelt in great detail on everything has gone wrong to derail the American Dream since the *Reagan Revolution* ended. You don't need a book to tell you the economy is in the tank, gasoline costs way too much, we are bogged down with a confused foreign policy and the country is infested with drugs and illegal aliens - uh, sorry, Undocumented Democrats.

As I noted above, my wife and her lady friends, like to *talk* about problems; while I *fix* them. Everything in America can be *fixed!* We will start with the fractured, immature, and angry, giant known as the tea party movement. With these new tea party allies, our Cavalry will ride to the rescue... we will next *fix* the Republican Party. *fix* started in the 2010 elections. We demanded a return to the principles of both our Party Platform, and the US constitution, which made America great, strong, and free. We demanded a line in the sand, and once more gave America a clear choice between freedom and socialism. America chose freedom!

Our brightest days are still ahead of us. America has always had the right program for freedom and economic prosperity. Our *moral guide* is found in the Ten Commandments. Our *vision quest* was the Declaration of Independence. Our *Mission Statement* is the constitution of the United States. Our detailed *business plan* is the platform of the Republican Party. America is once more on the comeback trail. The Republican Party has returned to its core mission of getting the government out of the way, so the people may, with Gods help, prosper. The next generation will live better, and have more opportunities, than we have enjoyed. There will be a rebirth of freedom, and economic opportunity, from sea to shining sea.

Freedom does not come quickly or without struggle and effort. There are no problems we cannot solve, but it will take hard work, wise choices, strong leadership, and better organization.

In the chapters follow, we examine what made America exceptional in the long history of the world. We examine the causes of our current malaise. We will outline a clear plan to return this republic once more to greatness. The tea party movement is playing a vital part in national resurgence. If you are reading this book because you understand the tea party movement, the Republican Party, and the United States of America, still have their best days ahead of them, welcome aboard the freedom train. Roll up your sleeves, and get ready to become organized, and go to work.

In the event you are a pessimist who does not believe these things can be done, I can scarcely improve upon the advice of Samuel Adams to your kind during the American Revolution.

"If you love wealth more than liberty, the tranquility of servitude better than the animating contest of freedom, depart from us in peace. We ask not your counsel nor your arms. Crouch down and lick the hand feeds you. May your chains rest lightly upon you and may posterity forget you were our countrymen."

Chapter One

America's First Tea Party!

Allow me to begin by resolving a dispute concerning the question of who held the first Tea Party in America and therefore has the best claim to the use of the name. That honor goes to Samuel Adams, Paul Revere, and 171 other *Mohawks* assembled at the *Green Dragon Tavern* in Boston, Massachusetts, in the days leading up to December 16, 1773.

The *British East India Company*, chartered by Queen Elizabeth I December 31, 1600, grew into what we now call a multi-national corporation. The *British East India Company* was responsible for much of the ascension to world dominance of the British Empire. Most of the manufactured goods used in the American colonies were delivered in ships owned or leased by the British East India Company. By the 1770's the American colonies and much of the world were suffering a decade long economic recession. Compounding the woes of the British East India Company, colonists now manufactured most of the goods once imported from elsewhere in the Empire. Tea was one of the few goods still imported in large amounts. Because of tax laws, much of tea was smuggled illegally from the Dutch rather than purchased legally from the British.

By early 1773, the *British East India Company* was on hard times and needed a financial bailout from Parliament, much like our recent government bailouts of big banks and automobile manufacturers.

The bailout, known popularly as the *Tea Act*, was passed May 10, 1773. The long title was *An act to allow a drawback of the duties of customs on the exportation of tea to any of his Majesty's colonies or plantations in America; to increase the deposit on bohea tea to be sold at the East India Company's sales; and to empower the commissioners of the treasury to grant licenses to the East India Company to export tea duty-free.*

The intended effect of the *Tea Act* would be to allow the British East India Company to sell 17 million pounds of tea in the American colonies more cheaply than the colonists could smuggle

Dutch tea. To some folks this looked like a good deal for everyone. It saved the *British East India Company* from financial ruin, unloaded 17 million pounds of poor quality tea stored in London, and allowed American colonists to buy tea at cheaper prices.

There was one problem with this financial bailout; it retained a small tax the Americans would pay on the tea. This tax was the last vestige of the *Townsend Act* of 1767, and asserted, as a principle, the Crown preserved the right to tax American colonists without allowing them any representation in Parliament. To make matters worse, revenue from the tax on tea defrayed the costs of Royal Governors and other officials in the colonies. This made those officers less responsive to the will of the local populace.

Seven ships loaded with tea were sent from England to America. One ship ran aground in bad weather. Colonists in Philadelphia and New York refused to allow the tea to be unloaded and the ships returned to England. In Charleston, South Carolina, the tea was unloaded but locked in warehouses and left to rot without the tax being paid.

In Boston Royal Governor Thomas Hutchinson refused to allow the ships to be sent back to England. The local patriots posted 25 armed guards on the wharf, under the command of Paul Revere, to see the tea was not unloaded. Governor Hutchinson refused to compromise because the tea trade in Boston included two of his own sons and a son-in-law who were the Royal Commissioners responsible for collecting the tax. British law required the ships to be unloaded and the tax paid within 20 days of arriving in port.

Dartmouth first of the three ships, would reach this deadline on the 17th of December. If the Patriots were going to take any action it would have to be no later than December 16th. The three ships *Dartmouth, Eleanor, and Beaver,* were American owned. *Dartmouth* was originally constructed as a whaler. Bostonian John Rowe, a Mason, and Grand Master of the St. John's Grand Lodge of Massachusetts (Moderns), owned the *Eleanor.*

Conspiracy buffs have speculated the Boston Tea Party, or even the whole American Revolution, was a Masonic conspiracy of some sort. The truth is much more complicated. As we will see, in

December of 1773, there were Masons among the Patriots dumping tea overboard, Masons among the ship owners importing the tea, and in England, Masons, including Ben Franklin, negotiating commerce with the colonies. A large number of the leading citizens in Boston were Freemasons; many of those were prominent leaders in the activities culminating in what would much later be called the Boston Tea Party.

Much has been made of the fact the tea party itself was planned, in some detail, at gatherings in the *Green Dragon Ta*vern. The St. Andrew's Masonic Lodge purchased the *Tavern* in 1764, and two Masonic Lodges held Communications at location. This fact alone does not prove much of anything. The *Green Dragon Tavern* was one of the largest buildings on the north Side of Boston in 1773 and numerous gatherings were held there, some Masonic, and many others not. The *Tavern* was more what we would describe as a community center today.

The tea party was a criminal act under British law; the tea destroyed was valued at roughly $1 million in modern dollars. These *Mohawks*, generally believed to have been about 173 in number, made an agreement among themselves not to reveal the names of participants for 50 years. Remarkably, almost all the participants kept pledge. Of the approximately 173 men, only about forty were known to be Masons and many more than number could have been.

Brother James Otis, a member of St. John's Lodge, is credited by historians with coining the phrase, *"Taxation without representation is tyranny!"* Dr. Joseph Warren, a Harvard educated physician, was made a Mason in 1761, and became Grand Master of Masons in Massachusetts in 1767. Warren was one of the guiding lights of the American Revolution. Among other things, Dr. Warren served as head of the Committee of Public Safety in Boston. With his Masonic Brother William Molineux, Dr. Warren tried vainly to convince John Rowe, owner of the *Eleanor* and a Brother Mason, to take his ship back to England.

When Paul Revere, later Grand Master of Masons in Massachusetts, made his famous midnight ride, it was done on the orders of Dr. Joseph Warren who was, in effect, spymaster of the colony. A rifle ball in the battle of Bunker Hill killed Warren, who had been commissioned as a Major General in the Massachusetts Militia, on 17 June 1775.

Col. Thomas Crafts, was an early member of the *Loyal Nine*, an organization later changed its name to *Sons of Liberty*. Crafts was a member of St. Andrew's Lodge F. & A.M. and an officer of the Grand Lodge of Massachusetts.

Masonic Lodges exist to teach the fatherhood of God and the brotherhood of man. They teach morality and brotherly love by means of allegory and symbols. While no atheist may be made a Mason, the Fraternity is not a religion, nor does it involve itself with politics. There are but two subjects forbidden to be discussed within the body of a Masonic Lodge, politics, and religion.

At the time of the Boston Tea Party, as it came to be called fifty years later, Brother Benjamin Franklin, Grand Master of Masons in Pennsylvania, was in London on business. When informed of the *destruction of the tea*, as it was known at the time, Franklin deplored the action, offering to pay for the tea out of his own pocket.

Thus we see prominent Masons involved in planning and carrying the tea party into execution. At the same time, at least one of the three owners of the ships carrying the tea was also a Mason, and the most famous Mason in America, Benjamin Franklin, was completely unaware of the plan, was appalled by it, and offered to pay for the destroyed tea. What is the most reasonable conclusion to be drawn from the known facts? There were numerous Masons prominent in New England society at time, but the Masonic Fraternity, as an organization, was not involved in any manner with planning or carrying out the destruction of the tea.

What did the *Sons of Liberty*, who met regularly at the *Green Dragon Tavern,* call the men who planned and carried out the first tea party in America? For whatever reason, they chose to call themselves *Mohawks*, some carried tomahawks and they even adopted a rather silly sounding password and countersign to identify each other. A *Mohawk* challenging a stranger would say "*Ugh!*" and the *Mohawk* so challenged would raise his tomahawk and say "*Me know you!*" whereupon the first *Mohawk* would also raise his own tomahawk in recognition and repeat "*Ugh!*"

These *Mohawks,* meeting in the *Green Dragon Tavern,* called their club the *Caucus Pro Bono Publico.* While many members of the club were Masons, others were not. One of the leaders of the *Sons of Liberty* and of the Boston Tea Party, Samuel Adams was never a Mason.

Most of these *Mohawks* were very young at the time they participated in the Tea Party. Samuel Cooper was only 16 when he helped with the destruction of the tea. Cooper would be commissioned as a Lieutenant in Washington's Revolutionary Army, fought in battles at Bunker Hill, Trenton, Brandywine, Germantown, Monmouth and would rise to the rank of Major. He lived to be 84 and is buried in Virginia. His youngest son and namesake would serve as Adjutant and Inspector General of the Confederate States of America with the rank of full General. George Robert Twelves Hewes, a shoemaker by trade, was 31 when he led one of the three boarding parties. He would live to age 98 and write one of the definitive books about the Tea Party, from which much of our knowledge today is derived. Hewes was not the oldest survivor of the Tea Party. That honor went to David Kinnison who lived to 115. The only man imprisoned for the tea party was Francis Akeley (or Eckley). The only man injured during the Tea Party was John Crane age 29, knocked unconscious by a falling chest of tea. Crane, a Mason, would rise to the rank of Brigadier General, and died in 1805. Amos Lincoln, a Mason, was 20 at the time he participated in the tea party. Lincoln subsequently rose to the rank of Lt. Colonel and married two of Paul Revere's daughters.

Not everyone who contributed to the success of the Tea Party actually boarded a ship to destroy tea. Over 7,000 people gathered on the night of December 16, 1773 in a meeting, which had been moved to the Old South Meeting-House, then the largest building in Boston. The firebrand of the Revolution, Samuel Adams, delivered an impassioned speech on American rights. When informed Royal Governor Thomas Hutchinson had refused to allow the ships to depart for England without unloading, Adams said, *This meeting can do nothing further to save the country.* This was a pre-arranged signal to the *Mohawks* in the gallery who slipped quietly away and staged the very first tea party in America.

In order to keep as many people as possible away from Griffin's Wharf where the *Dartmouth, Eleanor,* and *Beaver* lay at anchor, Adams continued his long speech. Following Adams, Dr. Thomas Young, then age 41, delivered an impassioned speech on the health hazards of drinking tea. This lecture is widely assumed to have been a ploy to keep as many people as possible away from Griffin's Wharf.

The actual tea party was nothing like any tea party you have seen on TV or participated in. While a crowd estimated at 2,000 watched from the Wharf, there were no speeches, no signs, no flags, no elected officials, no reporters and no candidates for office in attendance.

The *Mohawks* met briefly in the *Green Dragon Tavern;* later dubbed '*Headquarters of the American Revolution*' to blacken their faces with soot, and be assigned to one of three boarding parties. Most of these 173 men did not, contrary to popular belief, disguise themselves as Indians. Many did disguise their faces and a few wrapped themselves in blankets as protection against the cold.

Each party quietly boarded one of the three ships, under the nose of a 60 gun British Man-o-war. A leader of each party went directly to the Captain of the ship, demanded, and got, the keys to the ship. Working quickly and silently, they brought the chests of tea, each weighing between 100 and 400 pounds to the deck. The tea chests were beaten open with tomahawks, and tossed into the harbor. The men worked with great discipline and were careful to insure nobody took any of the tea. This was civil disobedience, not theft.

Some of the ship crews, many of whom were Americans, actually helped destroy the tea. In all, 342 chests of tea, with a total weight of 42 tons, valued at a million dollars in our current money, were dumped overboard. This was hard work and took three hours from 7:00 PM till almost 10:00 PM. When the deed was done the *Mohawks* were careful not to damage anything, and actually swept the decks of the ships before leaving.

Most Mohawks immediately left Boston because they were now wanted men. Years after the success of the American Revolution, very few Mohawks ever spoke of the destruction of the tea on the night of December 16, 1773. Many became very prosperous businessmen and feared the British East India Company could bring lawsuits for the value of the tea they destroyed.

The British closed the port of Boston and sent 10,000 troops to occupy the city of 20,000 people.

Chapter Two

We Started The Tea Party

In the early 1970's a political movement to oppose federal income taxes spread rapidly across America. As the decade of the 1970's drew to a close, many of these protestors began to call their activities *tea parties*. Like the modern tea party movement, these tax protests were largely ad hoc, disorganized, and drew together people with many different philosophies and a litany of grievances against the federal government.

Typical of these was a former lawyer in Anderson, South Carolina, the late Robert B. Clarkson II. His aggressive style of tax planning repeatedly got Mr. Clarkson, and his numerous clients, into hot water with the dreaded IRS. One of the founders of the South Carolina Libertarian Party, Robert Clarkson believed taxes were bad, and the IRS was evil. In order to build a political movement, composed largely of wage earners, he often employed humor and ridicule to allay the fears of his numerous followers.

One of the biggest fears the average American had in the late 1970's was the IRS might audit their tax return. Clarkson dispensed two pieces of advice *"Don't file any tax return."* and *"If you are audited, turn it into a tea party and have some fun with the agents."* An article from the Greenville News for November 27, 1979 described one of these early tea parties:

ANDERSON - More than 250 miles from the nearest harbor and without an Indian in sight, Robert B. Clarkson held his own version of the Boston Tea Party at his Concord Avenue residence Monday afternoon

Sipping sassafras tea and boasting of harassing the Internal Revenue Service, the Anderson Resident - a "Tax Rebel!" button pinned top his lapel - succeeded in cutting a planned IRS audit of his financial records to less than a minute.

"We took control of the situation, which is a move right out of the IRS manual," Clarkson said as a stunned IRS agent drove off from the bizarre scene, all pre-arranged by Clarkson.

"This was all just to make it tough on them...the way they normally make it for the person being audited.

A member of the anti-tax oriented Carolina Patriots, the local resident and a man he called an "unidentified witness" turned what began as a routine audit into a fiasco could have found a home amid the pages of the National Lampoon.

Clarkson, sipping hot tea symbolic of the Boston tax rebellion 200 years ago, first asked the auditor to sit on a "quite uncomfortable" plywood box while Clarkson and his witness sat in "nice comfortable" chairs. The chairs were arranged around a small round table in Clarkson's driveway. The auditor's chair was placed so it faced directly into the sun.

Once the IRS agent arrived, Clarkson and the witness asked her to join them in a brief prayer followed by the Pledge of Allegiance to a flag taped to a 2-foot long board.

"We thought we should open with a prayer and a Pledge," Clarkson said. "This is only right because we are true patriots."

Clarkson then informed the agent he was going to tape-record the audit interview. The agent said she could not allow without first getting the approval of her superiors and turned to leave.

As she walked quickly away to her car, Clarkson followed closely behind, rapidly snapping her picture. Smiling broadly as the agent drove away, Clarkson stood by his car, its bumper festooned with stickers reading: "Rebellion to Tyranny is Obedience To God" and "Down With Taxes" He seemed pleased with the performance.

"Here we are fighting for the same freedoms our forefathers fought for in 1776," he said.

Through the decade of the 1980's there were dozens of tax protest organizations all over the United States. The phrase *tea party* passed into the lexicon of these tax rebels as a verb describing any of several types of confrontation with IRS agents, most often audits or summons enforcement attempts. For the next thirty years 1979 - 2009 any reference to a *tea party* was a euphemism for confrontation with the Internal Revenue Service. A gradual tradition developed among Libertarian activists and tax protestors to hold public demonstrations, *tea parties*, around the country, usually on April 15th when tax returns were due.

The modern *tea party* as a public political demonstration against big government, high taxes and wasteful spending had its genesis in the actions of Samuel Adams, Paul Revere, and Dr. Robert B. Clarkson, but seems in 2009 to have occurred spontaneously to multiple political activists across the country in Hundredth Monkey fashion.

The story goes, scientists studying Macaques monkeys on Koshima, an island off the coast of Japan, decided to drop sweet potatoes on the beach as food for the monkeys. One day in 1952, a young female monkey named Imo learned her potatoes tasted better if she washed the sand off before eating them. She taught this skill to her mother, and to other monkeys. More and more monkeys learned to wash their potatoes from Imo and her friends. Then one day in 1958 a critical number was reached. Perhaps the number of monkeys with the new skill increased from 99 to 100 monkeys. With the hundredth monkey learning the behavior, something amazing happened, all the monkeys began to wash potatoes without having to learn the behavior. All the monkeys on the other islands began to wash potatoes, as did monkeys on the mainland of Japan. When a critical mass was reached, all the monkeys just knew the information without having to learn it.

Skeptics reviewed the data from Japanese scientists studying primates and attempted to debunk the theory. Theoretical Biologist Robert Sheldrake calls the phenomenon morphogenesis and postulates all our minds are sub-consciously connected. He cites a ten-year experiment at Harvard University where rats were trained to escape from a water maze. He relates each generation of rats was born with the ability to escape from the maze quicker than generations before them. Even more astonishing was the fact rats in laboratories all over the world were now being born with the ability to escape from the water maze quickly!

How does it work? What is the mechanism of the Hundredth Monkey Syndrome? I have no idea! I simply know it does work. In 2009 you and I saw an awesome example of the Hundredth Monkey principle in action when the tea party movement went viral - and not over the Internet, but in the streets of America.

For thirty years, patriotic tax protestors called their annual April 15th rallies *tea parties*. Suddenly in 2009 every conservative political activist in America spontaneously decided to create and participate in the modern tea party movement. The tea party's hundredth monkey may have followed thirty years of consciousness raising by several thousand tax-protestors.

Like tax protestors before them, followers of Congressman Ron Paul frequently invoked the Boston Tea Party in rhetorical calls for action against high taxes. They may have been a precursor to the paradigm shift culminating in tea parties, but appropriated the name *tea party* into their campaign decidedly retroactively.

The 2008 presidential campaign with probably the best claim to originating many modern tea parties would be of former Arkansas Governor Mike Huckabee. He was an early supporter of the Fair Tax, H.R. 25, proposal to replace the IRS, and the income tax, with a national retail sales tax of 23%. These Huckabee/Fair-Tax rallies had more the flavor of current tea parties, complete with hand-lettered posters and store bought flags. Contrary to the assertions of the far left, these tea parties were not a racist reaction to Barack Obama, who had not yet been elected. Most of their fire was directed at the IRS and the bailout proposals of Republican President George W. Bush! Mr. Obama would earn the ire of the tea party movement the following year with his push for socialized medicine, now known as Obamacare.

Greenville County (South Carolina) Young Republicans called for a reenactment of the Boston Tea Party on the banks of the Reedy River February 26, 2009 just over a month after the inauguration of Mr. Obama's regime. They hoped to draw two hundred people and planned to toss tea bags into the Reedy River in symbolic protest. More than 2,000 angry tea partiers mobbed the banks of the Reedy - far in excess of what the organizers anticipated. A few months later on tax day, April 17, 2009 The Young Republicans had a second tea party protest in front of the Bi-Lo Center. This time they drew 10,000 people!

So, next time you are involved with a tea party group and some local loudmouth starts nonsense about how this or "Tea Party" is the real McCoy and all the others are co-opting *his* movement; ask if he really was in Boston's *Green Dragon Tavern* before December 16, 1773 in a previous life?

Chapter Three

The Real Million-Man March

Three people who each have a claim to being the proverbial hundredth monkey serving as a catalyst of American politics, transforming those disorganized local rallies into a dynamic national movement. The three are TV personality Glenn Beck, former House Majority Leader Dick Armey, and Congresswoman Michele Bachmann of Minnesota.

Freedom Works, led by Armey, called for a protest on the national mall in front of the US Capitol building early in 2009. Glenn Beck picked up on the call for action, and endorsed the idea. All year long the call for protest was picked up, adopted, endorsed, and expounded upon by bloggers, websites, organizations and millions of ordinary people fed up with socialism.

On September 12, 2009 about 1.8 million Americans from every walk in life, converged on Washington, D.C. for the largest political protest in the history of the world. The people poured into Washington, D.C. from every state. There were also numerous *tea party* events day all around the country for folks who could not afford to travel to the District of Confusion.

In 1995 racist agitator Louis Farrakhan, head of the *Nation of Islam* movement, called for one million black men to converge on Washington, D.C. for a *hate America and blame the white man* rally Farrakhan euphemistically called the **MILLION MAN MARCH**. His turnout for the rally fell far short of the predicted million men. The National Park Service charitably estimated the crowd at 400,000 nowhere near even half a million men.

In a nation where political correctness is favored over the truth, denigrating the Million Man March in any way was a punishable offense. From that time forward the National Park Service was no longer allowed to issue estimates of the size for crowds at public gatherings in our capitol. What does a real Million Man March look like?

September 12, 2009 there were somewhere between 1.5 and 1.8 million Americans converging on the Capitol building to tell the liberal power elite we are mad as hell and not going to take it any more. Estimates of the crowd ranged from a low of 60,000 reported by some left wing media outlets, to more than 2.3 million claimed by some participants. The lower number was almost certainly a conservative estimate made before 9:00 AM when participants were just beginning to arrive on the Mall. Most reliable estimates placed the afternoon crowds at between 1.5 and 1.7 million. There may well have been 2.1 million who participated during some part of the day, but there were probably never more than 1.7 million people in the Capitol at the same time.

Like the first Tea Party in 1773, what actually matters, is not exactly how many people were there, but what did they accomplish of any lasting value? The great American tea party of September 12, 2009 was radically different from almost every other mass gathering in the long history of protests in our nation's capitol.

The most obvious difference was the demeanor of the participants. I arrived on Pennsylvania Avenue around 9:00 AM. I was on one of 8 busloads of citizens from Greenville, South Carolina who rode all night to be there. As we walked briskly down Pennsylvania Avenue for about a mile and a half, people streamed-in from every adjoining street as we passed, and the crowd swelled block by block.

The D.C. Police were out in force, dressed in full riot gear, with body armor, helmets, and heavy automatic weapons. Initially the Police were very abrupt, almost hostile to the demonstrators. It was as if the police had been told to prepare for violence, confrontations, and lawlessness. They would not engage in conversation and were a bit rude and arrogant when they gave an order to clear a sidewalk.

Over the next three or four hours, the attitude of the Police changed almost 180 degrees from the initial hostility. What happened over those three hours? They noticed, every time they gave an order to the crowd, everyone in earshot said, "*Yes sir!*" and cheerfully complied. They noticed many of us brought empty trash bags with us and policed up our own trash, rather than leaving anything on the ground. The D.C. Police had never seen demonstrators pick up their own trash! The folks present for the Obama Inauguration had left tons of garbage all over the National Mall and on many of the city streets. It had taken several days for city workers on overtime to clean up the massive mess the Obama supporters left.

The D.C. Police noticed our crowd included lots of families, women and children. They noticed, for the most part, those children were well behaved. There were no protesters carrying any sort of weapon; but a lot of them were carrying Bibles, and almost everyone had a copy of the US constitution. There were tens of thousands of homemade, hand-lettered, signs on several dozen different issues. None of those signs complained about law enforcement, and none of our people called them pigs. Thousands of times, people of all ages, and from all walks of life were going up to the officers, thanking them for their service to our nation and telling the police they were praying for their safety.

After three or four hours, it was sort of like Hundredth Monkey syndrome all over. The cops spontaneously figured out we were not in D.C. to cause trouble, and we actually appreciated them. They started allowing folks to shake hands with them, and pose for pictures next to them. By lunchtime, the Cops were giving advice on where the best places to eat were, or where the nearest bathroom was located.

Police officers who had been briefed to expect rioting and terrorists, now realized we were ordinary Americans. Not only were we not in town to make trouble or trash the place, we actually respected and appreciated law enforcement officers!

I would like to give you a list of all the speakers at the podium, and briefly summarize the main points of each talk. However, there were almost a million people between the speaker's platform and myself. Most of us could not hear much of what was being said at the podium. The amazing transformation in America that day did not come from the leaders on the platform. It happened spontaneously in the crowd. Every few minutes for almost nine hours, I heard someone around me in the throngs of people say what I had been thinking. It was something like *"Wow! There really are millions of people all over the United States who think just like me. I am not alone, and I am not really outside the mainstream - no matter what the national media says!"*

Over a million people began to spontaneously exchange contact information with each other. Many a local tea party was organized for the first time on the long bus ride home, including one right here in Greenville, South Carolina.

The term *tea party* was being transformed from a verb used to describe a public rally, to a noun used to describe an organization, would meet regularly, get organized, and start educating members on effective political action.

All day, at various times, someone would lead a chant among the 1.7 million people gathered on the National Mall in front of the Capitol building. The crowd would roar in unison *"Can you hear us now?"* a rhetorical question directed to the members of Congress and the regime in power. We were shouting outside government buildings and offices where our elected officials and bureaucrats worked every day. In reality, they did not hear us chanting, and news coverage of the oft-asked question *"Can you hear us now?"* was somewhat sporadic. On September 12, 2009 Congress, as a whole, had not yet heard our demands for lower taxes or less government spending – they would hear us on Election day.

Most of our hand-lettered signs were rather tame, and many in the crowd were of a religious bent and not inclined to any sort of vulgarity in language or signs. One sign was an exception to this general tenor of the event really did sum up the view of many. The sign read *"Obamacare: Cram it down our throats in 2009 and we will shove it up your ass in 2010."* This sign would prove very prophetic. Congress had not heard us yet, and they would go on to pass the massive 2,000 page plus, socialized medicine power grab federalizing roughly 18% of our national economy.

Chapter Four

Michele Bachmann Sounds the Alarm!

In the dark days following the 2008 election much of Middle America was in a state of shock and disbelief. The Democrat party, once almost a dead anachronism, had been resurrected like the fiend in a bad horror movie. Suddenly an anti-American racist with a Moslem upbringing had usurped the White House. Along with the man from Kenya, the Democrat Party and its many communist and socialist allies in organized labor had been dramatically swept into total control of the United States government.

In the run up to the 2008 general elections the establishment Old Guard, often derisively labeled as RINO's had been in almost total control of the GOP machinery. They could count among their number the Chairman of the RNC, Michael Steele, a majority of the RNC itself. In every state they set the tone, controlled the purse strings, and thereby the strategy, of the upcoming elections. The Old Guard paid lip service to the party platform but focused on justifying the socialist bank bailouts in the last days of the Bush administration. They also had a pathological fear of being seen as radical, or outside accepted orthodoxy as defined by the mostly liberal mainstream media and the academic pundits it touted as experts on all things normal.

The election results were predictable. The GOP got clobbered. We were buried in a socialist landslide. The demoralized rank-and-file grassroots of the Republican Party failed to turn out and vote. Even more damning, we failed to open our purses or contribute our blood, sweat, and tears, for candidates like John McCain. Candidates who steadfastly refused to attack the open socialists nominated by the Democrats. These were candidates who seemed ashamed of our values, beliefs, and principles; reluctantly defending those values tepidly, if at all.

On Election Day we, conservative Republicans, had been clobbered decisively in a landslide. As Middle America saw itself abandoned by a GOP which, even when out of power, had always been the loyal opposition to socialism, they were frustrated. That frustration boiled over as we lambasted our members of Congress for these failures in Town Hall meetings all over America. Soon the frustration simmering in Town Hall meetings was also manifested in similar vocal protests within the machinery of the GOP establishment. Conservatives rallied the troops in thousands of county conventions and county executive committee meetings all across America, but particularly in the Republican strongholds of the South and the Midwest.

It was this seething dissatisfaction by conservatives feeling betrayed, led directly to the rise of the tea party movement. As we have already noted above, at least in the beginning, the tea party movement, was largely a spontaneous outpouring of anger, and a demonstration of our frustration with betrayal by our own leaders. The early *Tea Parties* were mass demonstrations of folks who were, in the immortal words of the late Howard Jarvis, "*madder than hell and not going to take it any more!*"

As these sorts of protests swept the country in 2008-2009, a growing national consciousness developed for a march on Washington, D.C. to make sure our national leaders heard from the people loud and clear. This culminated, as we have discussed, on September 12, 2009 in the most massive political protest in the history of the world.

We all went to Washington, D.C. and gave the middle finger to the man from Kenya. Then we went home and congratulated ourselves for finally having become the mouse roared. We called in on talk radio, wrote largely unpublished letters to newspaper editors; and, continued to lambaste members of congress, including many Republicans, who were brave enough to continue to hold Town hall meetings.

In spite of this frenzy of national anger over big government, with its attendant high taxes and reckless spending, those who seized power in November of 2008 were hell bent upon using power to dismantle the nation we all grew up in and replace it with their own version of a socialist utopia. They unleashed an orgy of spending and borrowing unprecedented in the history of the world. The socialists, elected as Democrats, were in town expressly for the dual purposes, of looting the Treasury and transforming the American economy into a series of government managed, centralized bureaucracies. They focused on housing, banking, automobile manufacturing; and especially set their sights on the health care industry. The goal was to move boldly and quickly while they controlled all three branches of the federal government, nationalize medicine and everything related to it.

In the dark months after the debacle of the 2008 national election the *tea party* participants, and the few natural leaders who arose in their ranks, could think of nothing more than to continue to raise hell, complain, and point fingers, often including finger pointing at the Republican Party itself. There was lots of anger and not much intellect in many early leaders. They were more mob than political movement at that time. In fact, when a left wing critic called the *tea party* movement a *'mob'* the major talk radio station in South Carolina, WORD, printed and gave away tens of thousands of T-Shirts emblazoned with the slogan *"We are the MOB!"* Tea partiers snapped these up and they became the de rigueur uniform of the day for folks from the Upstate of South Carolina going to Washington, D.C. on September 12th 2009.

While our people in the streets waving rattlesnake flags and letting off steam took pride in being a disorganized mob; there were a few visionary leaders in the conservative movement who recognized things were about to get a whole lot worse; and the tea partiers in the streets, and calling the talk shows, were not stemming the tide of socialism. There is a big difference between being angry, frustrated, betrayed, alienated; and, actually having a plan to frustrate our enemies and reclaim power over our own lives, culture, and institutions.

One of those visionary leaders was Minnesota Congresswoman Michele Bachmann, a conservative leader who bucked the trend of Republican losses in the 2008 elections, being decisively re-elected from a very *'blue'* state. Rep. Bachmann understood the left was steamrolling a massive 2,000 page bill through Congress. A bill almost no one had read!

If this medical reform bill, dubbed Obamacare, made it into law the America we all grew up in was doomed to extinction. This was more than just a power grab for the feds to seize control of almost 1/5th of our economy. The new "entitlement" would be created would create a massive and unavoidable tsunami of debt in the future. Debt that will downgrade our credit rating, devalue our currency, and, eventually, sink our whole economy under an unsupportable mountain of red ink.

The attractive Minnesota Congresswoman, mother of five, and foster mother of another 23 children, was one of the very few people in America to actually read the text of the bill. House Speaker Nancy Pelosi famously quipped we just needed to "*pass the bill now so we can find out what is in it!*"

Michele Bachmann knew what was in it, and the dark knowledge was frightening indeed. Bachmann understood the Democrats in congress were doing an end run around the usual legislative appropriation machinery in place. Among other things, Obamacare included $105 billion dollars in pre-approved funding for the first year of implementation alone, and billions more for future years. That meant, if this nightmare power grab happened, the left had positioned themselves to push this monstrosity into the very fabric of our nation even if they were to later lose majority control of congress.

Michele Bachmann began to warn the Republican leadership, her fellow Republicans in congress, and the American people; this bill was a monstrosity that needed to be derailed if we were to save our republican government and free market based health care system.

She called for another massive march on Washington, this time, the march would be focused like a laser beam on stopping Obamacare and exposing the enormity of what was actually being proposed as the centerpiece of the Obama regime in Washington. Talk radio hosts Glenn Beck, Rush Limbaugh, and Laura Ingram took up her call. Bachmann became a modern Paul Revere riding, mostly over the airwaves, to worn every community in America socialism was coming under the name Obamacare. She asked the American people to once again come to Washington, DC and make their voices heard on this legislative scheme. The date set was November 5th 2009

The word went out over the airwaves, through Internet based social networks, via telephones tweets and texts, and in a thousand local tea party gatherings in communities large and small, all over this land. The people were going back to Washington and we were going to tell the looters in government to get their hands out of our pockets and leave the greatest medical system in history alone. Medical care in America is not broken - Congress is broken.

Less than two months after the massive September 12th national tea party, we were all back in the capitol. This time, we were not just mad at big government in general. Thanks to the tireless efforts of Michele Bachmann, we were in town to take on, and defeat, the centerpiece of the Obama revolution. We were there to stop Obamacare. Not to improve it, not to compromise over it, but to drive a stake through the heart of the monster.

Bachmann was joined on the steps of our national capitol by all 179 Republican Members of Congress, actor John Voit, and dozens of national leaders in the burgeoning *tea party* movement; and by almost a half million ordinary Americans, including this author. She patiently explained to the cheering crowd how Obamacare, if left unchecked would fundamentally change America forever - and the change would be in the direction of less care, death panels, higher taxes, rationed care, and a future debt would first cripple, then destroy our nation.

In September, we went to Washington to express our frustration and to blow off steam. Now, in November, we were no longer disorganized, leaderless, protesters. We were the beginnings of an army. We were now an army that was focused on a specific legislative agenda. An army ready to defeat any Member of Congress who voted wrong on this and other matters that involved fiscal responsibility and constitutional principles. To all outward appearances, this rally was a carbon copy of the September demonstration, there were, once again, flags, speeches, signs, and lots of folks who were very angry about the abuses Obama and his crowd were inflicting on our nation when they were not busy flying around the world apologizing for America.

Many in the fledgling tea party movement prided themselves on having no leaders. They actually liked being a ship with no rudder. Some who embraced this almost communal idea of a proletarian movement similar to the Chinese Red Guards in the mid 1960's had a variety of reasons. Some feared taking on responsibility because they would have to actually get something done, which is much harder than just complaining. Others feared if there were leaders, they would not rise into those ranks. Still others, justifiably angry at the failure of American culture and institutions, particularly the Republican Party, wanted all these institutions to be replaced.

As the individual tea parties continued to squabble about whether they should have leaders or not; responsible conservative leaders were quick to tap into the anger and determination of millions of Americans that things must change. Michele Bachmann formed the *Congressional Tea Party Caucus*, it quickly grew as 66 Members of Congress joined.

Some in the various tea parties have resented her leadership and even gone so far as to say Bachmann was trying to usurp a position they were militant must not ever be filled - leader of the Tea Party. What they failed to grasp was Bachmann had no desire to take over the street level tea parties all across America. Like a lot of other movement conservatives in the decades before her, Bachmann was what TV commentator Bill O'Reilly has dubbed a Culture Warrior. She understood the America we loved and grew up in was under vicious attack by the far left. To win battle, we would need to fight for control of congress itself. We would need to raise, and spend, a lot of private money in defense of free enterprise and our American way of life.

Bachmann understood these things so well Nancy Pelosi once more made her top priority in the coming 2010 election the defeat of Congresswoman Michele Bachmann.

Michele Bachmann raised more money, $13 million dollars, than any Congressman running for re-election had ever done in history. The people of Minnesota re-elected Bachmann in a landslide. As for leadership of the tea party movement, Michele Bachmann had no interest in any title, nor did she seek to tell anyone what to do. She simply wanted the millions of angry, but energetic, tea partiers, to know they did not have to batter down the gates of power, Bachmann and the other movement conservatives in the Republican Party were going to open those doors from the inside and welcome the tea partiers to a place at the table as the strategy for saving America is hammered out.

It would take another year for these plans to bear fruit, but tea party was no longer a verb describing revolution and protest. It now became a noun describing a movement that would take power and dominate the next session of Congress.

Chapter Five

Conservative Victory

In spite of the massive protests in Washington in response to the call of Michele Bachmann, and the overwhelming opposition of the American people, Obama and the Democrat controlled congress passed the Obamacare bill.

The outrage of the American people was quick and pervasive. The Attorneys general of twenty six states sued the federal government over the constitutionality of the mandates contained in the Obamacare monster and several federal courts have already struck down major provisions of the bill as unconstitutional; particularly the federal mandate to purchase health insurance.

The tea parties, once harmless courthouse protests, now began crash courses all over America to learn how the machinery of the Republican Party worked and get involved. The far left was apoplectic because the GOP was actually going to stop compromising, grow some gonads, and really fight for its principles, for a change.

Embattled movement conservatives welcomed the new blood provided by the tea party movement and began showing them the ropes. Soon there was new life infused into the Republican Party. We were once more championing free enterprise, rather than government, as the solution to problems. More importantly, very conservative community leaders stepped forward and offered themselves as candidates for public office. Due, at least in part, to the vigorous support of the new 'tea party' Republicans now active in precincts across America, constitutional conservatives began to win primaries.

The establishment, the media, and the far left, began to chant a mantra in unison *"GOP nominees are too far right"* the left predicted we could not *"win in November."* Well, as Ronald Reagan used to say, the problem is what our opponents *"know that just isn't so."* With a few exceptions on the Senate side, tea party backed, movement conservatives won and won big in the 2010 election. We gained firm control of the House of Representatives, electing 87 tea party freshmen, and Nancy Pelosi would no longer be Speaker of the House.

Gaining the Senate in 2010 was always a long shot for Republicans; we did pick up some seats with solid conservatives like Pat Toomey in Pennsylvania; and libertarian Rand Paul in Kentucky.

The GOP had been *re-branded* to borrow a word from the world of corporate advertising. We were once more the party of limited government, morality, strong national defense, and free enterprise, as we had been under Ronald Reagan. The 2010 election clearly showed, once more, the theory there is a mass of undecided, independent, middle of the road voters, waiting to vote for indecisive candidates with a lukewarm plan, is simply a fiction completely divorced from reality.

The reality is strong leaders, offering a clear message, even if the message is only *"hope & change"* will win every time over the moderate middle-of-the-roader who does not clearly offer any vision for the future. Barack Obama won by running to the left of Karl Marx as an open racist in Rev. Wright's pews, and he openly espoused socialism. As he told Joe the Plumber, we need *"wealth redistribution!"*

Strong leaders, of either the right, or of the left, win elections. Folks in the muddled middle, running on socialism-lite, routinely go down in flames as has been proven numerous times with candidates like Bob Dole and John McCain.

In 2010 Republicans largely rejected the bad advice to tone down the message of freedom and limited government. We followed the axiom of conservative icon Barry Goldwater and gave the voters *"A choice not an echo!"* The American people clearly chose the tea party assisted, re-branded, full-bodied, red blooded, conservative program of the new GOP.

Chapter Six

Why Lefties Hate the T-Party

Why does the far left, and its lap-dog media cronies, hate the tea party movement so vehemently?

Is it because they want to raise taxes and we do not?

Is it because they favor "*affirmative action*" and we do not?

Because they support organized labor and we do not?

They hate guns, and we love them?

They want more debt and we want less?

They kill babies and we don't?

They think homosexuals should marry and we know marriage is ordained of God?

They want open borders and we want law enforcement?

They are anti-Semitic and we are not?

We venerate the constitution and they ignore it?

All these things and a thousand other issue related subjects are each small contributors to the stark differences between the tea party movement and the far left. All these issues combined are not what drive the far left into fits of irrational rage. There is one big lie they have cultivated for over a half-century which many Republicans bought into. The tea party movement threatens to unravel the dogmatic acceptance of one big lie can drive the far left from power once and for all.

Adolph Hitler knew the secret. Barack Obama knows the secret and uses it. Joe Stalin knew the secret. The secret all three knew and used is this: Tell a big enough lie, tell it often enough, and you will fool millions of people into believing the lie.

What big lie does the far left fear the tea party movement will expose?

Here is the big lie, as they usually tell it:

"In American politics, people on the extremes of the political spectrum usually nominate the candidates of the Democrat and Republican parties, but general elections are won - or lost - by the big, lukewarm, undecided, mass of militant non-committalists in the center. To win elections, you must water down your message, compromise on your principles, and become moderate."

Pay attention: **Nobody on the far left has ever followed this silly advice because they know it does not work!** No Democrat since Grover Cleveland has ran for office as a 'moderate.' Woodrow Wilson embraced the League of Nations, FDR ushered in massive, and often unconstitutional state socialism. Harry Truman ordered radical for the time, racial integration of the Armed Forces, and allowed the United Nations to trump General Douglas MacArthur's plans to win the war in Korea. John Kennedy screwed up, the Bay of Pigs, race relations, and the war in Vietnam. He almost got us into a war over Cuba, backed down before Kruschev's bluff, and secretly agreed to remove US intermediate range nuclear missiles from Turkey. Kennedy also promised to leave communist dictator, and Soviet puppet, Fidel Castro in power in Cuba, dooming millions of Cubans to decades of communist slavery.

Lyndon Johnson, Jimmy Carter, and Bill Clinton were each hard line leftist ideologues totally committed to looting the treasury to reward minorities, unions, socialists, and every species of anti-American trash. Lyndon Johnson explained the reason for his appointment of Thurgood Marshall to the United States Supreme Court by saying:

"Son when I appoint a nigger to the Court, I want everybody to know he is a nigger!"

Robert Caro pointed out in his extensive biography of LBJ, shortly after signing the 1964 Civil Rights Act, in a phone conversation (on tape at the LBJ Library) with Senator Richard

Russell of Georgia, LBJ said, "*That'll keep the niggers voting Democrat for the next 200 years.*"

The Democrat Party and the far left media have understood for a hundred years you win elections by making clear promises to your base of supporters; and then moving heaven and hell, once elected, to get them privileges and above all taxpayers money.

There is nothing the least bit "moderate" or indecisive, or middle-of-the-road about any of the policies they pursue. There is nothing moderate, or diverse, or inclusive, or middle of the road about Chuck Schumer, Jesse Jackson, Hillary Clinton, Jerimiah Wright, Bill Ayers, Al Sharpton, or Barney Frank. They are each far left radical ideologues bent on the destruction of America, as we have known it.

The Democrat Party does not even pretend to be *moderate*, or to compromise on any part of its far left radical ideology. In spite of this fact, they persist in giving advice to Republicans, our path to electoral success should be found by abandoning our core principles, moving to the left, and appealing to this mythical block of indecisive 'independents' who will somehow embrace us, if only we are not too pure or too principled.

The truth is, even in general elections, the folks who have very little understanding of, or interest in, politics, are not very passionate about turning out. When they do vote, they are not looking for folks from either side with muddled views can be sold as *moderate* positions. The undecided voter is looking for a strong leader who is promising a clear result. The undecided voter will vote for a Ronald Reagan, or, for a Barack Obama, provided the candidate is promising he can clearly solve problems and produce results.

The stupidest thing the Republican Party can possibly do in a general election is to shoot itself in the foot by nominating boring candidates without clear beliefs and the passion to explain and defend those views.

The far left hates the *tea party* movement because movement clearly demonstrated folks who stand on principles not only win Republican primaries, in almost every case they also go on to win the general election once nominated. What the *tea party* movement has done is to clearly demonstrate the proposition a nominee must be 'moderate' to win general elections is simply not true.

All the pundits, professors, and professional prognosticators predicted the tea party movement would be a disaster for the GOP in 2010 because they were going to nominate strong supporters of free enterprise and constitutional limits on government. Those nominees would not be seen as moderate enough to attract votes from this mythical mass of middle-of-the-road voters. We nominated solid conservatives anyway and those conservatives wracked up decisive victories.

Even the few conservative losses in 2010 general elections were not honestly attributable to the conservative philosophy of the candidates who lost. We narrowly lost a US Senate race in California simply because state now has a LOT more Democrats than Republicans registered to vote. California, for the foreseeable future is going to be an uphill battle for any Republican running state wide, no mater if they are seen as moderate or conservative.

In Delaware we lost because our candidate told the public she used to dabble in Witchcraft! Not exactly the way to mobilize and turn out the Christian fundamentalists needed to elect any Republican. Neither of those losses can be blamed on the *tea party* movement, or on the philosophical positions those candidates held on important issues.

Chapter Seven

10 Reasons the Establishment Dislikes Tea Parties

What is the number one reason the GOP establishment dislikes tea parties? They are disliked because the *tea party* supporters often come on like a Bull in a China Shop. The establishment, in many cases, has a valid criticism of the tea party movement. Politics is a well organized game with precise rules and traditions which should be respected. Many of these rules are based upon requirements of the law, while others are customs and usages that have grown hoary with age; and, in most cases, should be respected. In all too many instances *tea party* supporters walked into meetings with the proverbial chip-on-the-shoulder and assumed everyone in the room is an enemy *'unless I know them to be one of us.'*

When guilty of this mistake, *tea party* supporters rapidly find themselves with opposition, or at least with folks irritated at them. This irritation usually does not spring from philosophical differences. Pure and simple, the tea party members have not bothered to learn the rules, understand the customs, find out who their natural allies are, and generally have failed to do their homework. You would never go to a baseball or football game and start a chant of *"Hole-in-*one!" *"Hole-in-one!"*

When you enter a country club luncheon, or an executive committee meeting on a college campus, manners, decorum, and a deep understanding of the rules and culture of American politics will win you more friends and allies than a passionate - but out of order - defense of your principles. I started this chapter with the number one pet peeve of the establishment, because it is the biggest *tea party* error. It is an error can be easily corrected simply by doing research and learning how to behave in a given circumstance. Failure to take the time to learn these things is the political equivalent of intentionally shooting yourself in the foot.

The second area of friction between the establishment, and the *tea party* adherents, stems from the fact tea partiers, for the most part, are green as a Christmas tree. The political establishment in general, and the Republican Party in particular, is an arena where gray hair and long service to the institution are venerated, if not actually worshiped. Tell them what you did for the Ronald Reagan campaign in 1980. Then do not be disappointed when they are not impressed. They want to know what your great-grandfather did for Theodore Roosevelt! This is somewhat less of a problem in the South since almost the entire Republican Party here did not exist prior to about 1964.

On my first trip to Charleston over thirty years ago, a dear sweet elderly little lady explained to me, only partly in jest, Charleston, South Carolina was where the Ashley River, and the Cooper River, came together to form the Atlantic Ocean! A less charitable friend compared Charlestonians to Orientals, he said, *"They eat rice and worship their ancestors."*

It is easy to see why most folks in South Carolina followed the late Senator J. Strom Thurmond into the Republican Party. Most of those humorous caricatures of Charleston are just as apt if applied to the Republican Party anywhere in America.

Tea party supporters will do very well for their cause if they understand the GOP has for decades tended to nominate presidential candidates based upon whose turn it is rather than whose ideas they like the most. At the presidential level, strategy has not worked particularly well. The party supported Gerald Ford over Ronald Reagan in 1976. They nominated both Bob Dole, and John McCain, long after each Senator should have been retired from politics rather than carrying our standard into battle.

Never the less, the GOP is very oriented to seniority and generally believes loyalty must be earned by long decades of faithful service, not just a few years. The tea party needs to do a much better job of understanding the culture you have stepped into!

Is there a case to be made for getting away from some of this fanatical dedication to seniority and whose turn has finally arrived? Sure! However, change will have to arrive gradually and through an orderly process. That culture is indeed, at long last, starting to change just a bit. The change will be accomplished by a generational changing of the guard, rather than with quick bull-in-a-china-shop confrontations.

The third complaint insiders have about the newbies from the *tea party* movement has to do with the *tea party* getting bad publicity. Again, the hidebound GOP establishment always prefers, whenever possible, to avoid confrontation, conflict, and publicity, much less *bad* publicity. Here, in many instances, the *tea party* crowd is getting a bad rap. The media is much more liberal than even the most RINO of our Republican brethren, and they are going to always pick out folks within the GOP fold, whom they can ridicule and pick on.

Tea party people, often are their own worst enemies. Everyone who is new to politics must have a baptism by fire from the media sooner or later. It is a rite of passage in the game of politics. I recall working on the paid staff of a candidate for president in 2007. We were at a Bronze Elephant dinner in Spartanburg, one of the largest counties in South Carolina. I had specifically instructed my candidate to position himself outside the banquet hall and try to personally greet and shake hands with as many voters as possible when they entered the building.

After a few minutes, I noticed our candidate was buttonholed by a reporter for the biggest left wing rag newspaper in the state. I sent one of our interns over to remind the candidate he was supposed to be meeting and greeting voters and over a hundred voters had walked by while our candidate was monopolized by the reporter. The candidate gave me an irritated look and continued to talk to the reporter, who was taking copious notes in shorthand.

Finally I tried to pry our candidate away from the reporter. The candidate rebuffed my attempt and glared at me with his best frown silently conveyed his thoughts *You are hired help, and I am doing a major interview with a big shot reporter, shut up and leave me alone!*

When I finally managed, a few minutes later, to pry him away from the reporter, I asked calmly *"Did you notice the slim, dark haired man who walked past you a minute ago as you were wrapping up your big interview?"* The candidate, excited about his own in depth interview, replied *"not really."*

"Well, 's too bad" I said. *" That man you ignored is a friend of mine and I wanted to introduce you."* My candidate, still a bit irritated with me, said *"Who was your friend and why is he so important I should cut short an interview just for him?"*

I replied, *"My friend's name is Mark"* I went on to explain he was Mark Sanford, and, at the time, the very popular Governor of South Carolina. The candidate was still a bit miffed at me, and I knew it.

The next day, we eagerly grabbed up a print edition of the big time newspaper. We found the story about the Bronze Elephant dinner on page five of section two, below the fold. The article the big shot reporter had written was only five inches. It just said, local Republicans gathered for $100 a plate B-B-Q and there were a few second tier presidential candidates present. The article went on to note, *"the highlight of the evening was a speech by Governor Mark Sanford."* They quoted a few lines from Sanford's speech and did not mention even the names of any of the would-be presidential candidates!

My candidate sheepishly apologized to me. He had been entertaining visions of how this important reporter's story - all about him and his views - was going to be splashed on the front page of the newspaper. The reality was this reporter was a junior man in his office who got stuck with assignments like having to work on a Saturday evening. The reporter knew very well what ever he wrote was going to face a liberal editor who would cut it down as much as possible and run it on an inside page. The reporter, a liberal himself, was merely *interviewing* my candidate because he was bored with the whole event, there because he had to be, and he found my candidate mildly amusing.

Sooner or later, every conservative in politics learns one of the big facts of life. The news media is the enemy. All interviews that are not live TV are a waste of time. Sarah Palin had to learn not to spend hours with Katie Couric. Eventually, the local tea party organizers and would be leaders grow up and understand the media is the enemy and they are certainly no exception to this rule. Don't talk to reporters, the rule should be carved in stone.

One of the best things you can do for your country, and for the conservative movement, is to never, ever, talk to reporters. When you must send them information, send written press advisories before the event and written press releases after the event. Don't talk to reporters! They are not going to write favorably about you.

The fourth reason the establishment dislikes the tea party people, was touched on in the last chapter. You have slaughtered a sacred cow of the establishment. For decades Rockefeller Republicans [That's what they were before someone coined the now current acronym RINO] preached we needed to nominate candidates who were moderate, temperate, boring, and only lukewarm about the Republican Party platform. Otherwise, we would alienate independent voters who were supposed to have the power to swing elections dramatically in one direction or the other. We were supposed to choose our words carefully, walk on eggshells, and never strongly defend our principles, lest we alienate these fickle independent voters.

Lots and lots of otherwise educated people with good common sense bought into this lie, year after year, they sometimes passed over good candidates because the establishment was fearful principled conservative candidates might scare away the independent voter.

The Republican left loved to gloat over the defeat of Barry Goldwater in 1964 and cite that single election as proof of the goofball theory about independents swinging elections one way or another. They conveniently forgot to mention 1964 was an anomalous situation because someone [more likely several some ones] had just blown John F. Kennedy's head off on national TV in Dallas Texas. Barry Goldwater was not running against Lyndon B. Johnson any more; he was running against a two year old John F. Kennedy, Jr. saluting his father's flag draped casket.

First Obama in 2008, and then the *tea party* movement in 2010, clearly proved if independents show up and vote at all, they actually tend to vote for the most radical candidates - whether of the right, or, of the left - provided those candidates show strong leadership, make clear promises, lay out a specific plan to solve problems, and get things done!

It turns out *independent* voters are not much different from liberals and conservatives; they are not looking for the wishy-washy, lukewarm candidate being careful not to offend them. Independent voters want to see a strong leader who knows what he is trying to do, and has an understandable plan to get there. John McCain ran as the moderate, don't rock the boat or offend the independents candidate. Barack Obama ran as the strong leader with a clear plan to bring hope and change. The independents did indeed vote for Obama. They voted for Obama, the *radical*, in spite of John's McCain's carefully choreographed *moderation*.

They voted for the candidate who came across as a strong leader who seemed to know what he was doing and could say what he believed in. Fortunately for Republicans, independent voters, like everyone else in America, can see when they have made a mistake. In the 2010 election independent voters were almost all in the GOP column, helping us retake the House of Representatives.

After all this empirical evidence from the last two elections, the *tea party*, and Barack Obama, have each shown clearly the way to get independent votes is to nominate a strong leader who will fight like hell for what he believes in. All this stuff about lukewarm candidates without strong views appealing to independent voters, or anyone else, is so much balderdash! The *tea party* proved it on 2010 and the RINO establishment hates them now. The RINO's can no longer sell all that warm manure about the appeal of moderates to independent voters. Probably without realizing it, this is a bigger victory for the tea party movement than even recapturing the people's house in 2010 was.

The fifth way the tea party alienates the establishment is by demanding strict adherence to principles. For many decades establishment practitioners of politics saw it as a game about who got what. They prided themselves in being able to wheel and deal and make compromises. We give you something, but clearly expect a *quid pro quo*. The new folks from the tea party come into the room, sometimes as newly elected officials, and say, we are going to do everything 100% by the constitution. Nothing infuriates a person without any solid convictions more than having to be seen next to someone with absolute convictions. The comparison is never flattering and the establishment is thereby stripped of the veneer of respectability.

The sixth way *tea partiers* irritate the establishment is our stubborn demand for actual results. Everybody in American politics can read poll numbers. Every one of them, including RINO's Democrats, socialists, and even communists, are absolutely in favor of having a balanced budget - someday. Us knuckleheads from the *tea party* are brash upstarts who actually demand a balanced budget now, not ten years from now

The establishment politicians, including a lot of Republican incumbents, will tell you a half a trillion dollar deficit is a great thing and shows how conservative he or she actually is. When you ask them to explain this amazing assertion, they reply *"The Democrats were going to borrow a trillion dollars from the red Chinese and we are only borrowing half much."* They assert, *"We saved you half a trillion off what they were going to spend!"*

That's sort of like explaining to your wife, you are confronted by six gang-bangers who want to rape her, and you have convinced them only three should rape her. Folks in the *tea party* movement want real results and want those results now, not over the next ten years. When you, in the *tea party* movement, promise or demand results - now - you are making it painfully obvious that incumbents, including quite a few Republican incumbents, have not been producing the results the people want. Is it any wonder only 9% of Americans have a favorable impression of Congress according to the latest Rasmussen Poll?

Reason number seven the establishment despises the tea party? They are not "team-players."

Reason number eight the establishment hates tea partiers. They will not support the re-nomination of RINO incumbents who generally are not guided by either the US constitution nor the Republican Platform, when making decisions and casting votes. For decades the RNC raised money by giving conservative speeches to the faithful about the need to stand up for our principles. They made those speeches at our Bronze Elephant Dinners (up North, they have "Lincoln Day" dinners, same basic thing). Then, the RNC quietly gave money to a lot of rotten liberals like Senator Arlen Specter, who was usually a reliable vote for the Democrat Party any time they really needed him.

The establishment hates the *tea party* movement for exposing the hypocrisy of this sort of thing. Even worse, tea partiers are asking increasingly *"Why do we need to send money to the RNC at all? Can't we just give money directly to the candidates we support?"* The answer is, of course, we can give money directly to candidates. As more and more of us do so, the party establishment and organizations like the RNC lose power and became much less relevant to the process.

Because of these changes, the ninth reason the establishment dislikes the *tea party* movement is because they are perceived as lacking party loyalty. This complaint is closely related to tea partiers being green and really not understanding the political process. Many tea party members, brand new to politics, fail to understand the Republican Party actually serves a number of very important functions which are necessary to preserve our conservative values and principles. Those newest to the process, and most frustrated with the crumbling of the America we all grew up in, have sometimes made brash statements about seeing the Republican Party as part of the problem and wanting to dismantle or replace the party rather than reform it.

To my tea party friends who think that way, and there are a lot of them, I have a word of advice. Consider the Republican Party to be sort of like a brand new limousine which is very fine, has luxury finish, a powerful engine, and all the extras that can be put on any motor vehicle. However, it also has two flat tires and an empty gasoline tank. You would never think of abandoning the limousine, much less setting it on fire. You would change the two flat tires and re-fill the gas tank. I cannot raise any defense for some of the shortcomings of the GOP.

I am reminded of Winston Churchill's statement about democracy. He is reported to have said, in a speech to the British House of Commons November 11, 1947, *"No one pretends democracy is perfect or all-wise. Indeed, it has been said democracy is the worst form of government except all those other forms that have been tried from time to time."* That is exactly the way I feel about the Republican Party. When the *tea party* is fighting to defend our freedom and our liberties, they must be careful not to throw away one of our most effective tools for that purpose, the Republican Party. You do not throw away a dull knife you sharpen it!

The tenth and final complaint establishment Republicans have about the tea party movement is how incredibly fractured and disorganized the movement is. The *tea party* phenomenon of 2009 did indeed rise largely from the grassroots. Unlike almost every other major movement in American history, it was not the result of any one man or group of men. It was not focused around any one issue. This movement is more of a recognition our nation has headed in the wrong direction, our institutions have broken down, our sources of education and information have been preempted by our adversaries, and, to be blunt, America is in a hell of a mess.

Under these rather unique circumstances, ordinary citizens, who have never involved themselves in politics, have stepped up to the plate and said *"I am willing to fight for what I believe in and I am willing to suffer what ever is necessary to save my country so my grandchildren will have the same freedoms and the same opportunity I have enjoyed."*

That is indeed a very noble, selfless, and patriotic attitude. I am absolutely confident God himself has raised many of you up, in answer to our prayers, for the purpose of liberating and reclaiming this nation from the forces of darkness symbolized by the Democrat Party and its cohorts in academia and the mass media.

With that acknowledgement out of the way, the tea party will not succeed until and unless it gets organized and learns how to fight effectively. I assume if you are still reading, you are ready to do just that, get better trained and organized, so you can start winning battles.

As a child, I was raised in a home where I went to Church. My only choice in the matter was whether I went to Church before, or after, my Momma tore up the seat of my pants if I balked at the suggestion.

The grown ups were fond of asking children *"What is your favorite story in the Bible?"* It took me a long time to formulate an answer to question. Eventually, I not only had a favorite story, I knew where to find it, I could re-tell the key points of it; and, I could explain why it was my absolute favorite.

Put this book down. Go get your Bible. Turn to the Sixth and Seventh Chapters of the book of Judges. Read my favorite story, it is there. Pay careful attention to the key points. How did God deal with Gideon? How did Gideon deal with volunteers? How many were selected to go into battle? What was the selection process?

How did God use those selected to deliver Israel from her enemies? What lesson do you find in my favorite story is applicable to the *tea party* movement of today?

Chapter Eight

Organize Your Tea Party Better

We have seen the *tea party* movement is not so much an organization, nor even a group of organizations, as a spirit of freedom that has swept the nation like an old-fashioned tent revival. That spirit is once more reminding our leaders, and those whose function is to mould public opinion, this nation was founded on some fundamental principles that have stood the test of time. This movement has been a sometimes-unwelcome reminder to those in high places; the maladies afflicting our republic in this generation are largely the fruit of abandoning many fundamental principles made America great.

Has the *tea party* movement swept through your town? What does it take for you to become a participant in the *tea party* movement? Are you a patriotic American who cares deeply about the future of our nation? Do you absolutely believe in free markets and in limited government as established in the US constitution? Those of you who answered yes to both questions are already a part of the tea party spirit sweeping America.

In the unlikely event there is not already one or more tea party oriented organizations in your area you might consider starting one. The tea party movement is unlike almost every other major institution in the world. You do not need permission to form a *tea party*. You do not need any license from the government. You are not required to be organized in some specific manner. There is no union you must join and no litmus test you must pass.

In fact, you don't even have to call your group a *Tea Party* unless you just want to. As Will Shakespeare wrote in Romeo and Juliet, a rose by any other name will smell just as sweet. The choice is yours. Call your group a *Tea Party* and people immediately identify you with the recent history of movement and all the good and bad associations the name brings to mind. You do not really need to do much explaining about who you are, or what you believe, as you start your recruiting program.

On the other hand, there are quite a few *Tea Party* groups in this country have fallen into the poor habit of bickering with each other. Some *Tea Parties* accusing others of deviating from orthodoxy, or even of *"hijacking"* the name from others more deserving of the right to use it. Does it make any difference if you call your group the *Wilson County Tea Party?* Or if you call your organization the *Wilson County Constitutional Study Group?* A rose by any other name will smell just the same.

There is no wrong way to fight the cancer of big government other than to be ineffective. Remember, the reason to get organized, educated, and trained, is simply to become more effective, nothing more or less.

Have a clear purpose! The most important thing is for you to have a very clear purpose. What are you trying to accomplish. Be very specific so people understand what you are asking them to help you accomplish. *"Make the Republican Party more conservative"* is an ambiguous platitude which does not tell your members and the community at large what you are about.

Here is an example of a very specific purpose: *"Replace every Republican Congressman in this state who voted for the TARP Bank Bailout Bill."* it happens to be a goal we accomplished in South Carolina in 2010! It was hard work. There were hundreds of volunteers involved. We even took on a popular and well-funded Congressman, Gresham Barrett, running for Governor. Because Barrett voted for TARP in congress, we did not want him as Governor.

Because of his connections to the banking and financial institutions he helped bail out, Barrett started as the odds on favorite to win the nomination for Governor in a five way race. First we forced him into a runoff and then we defeated him soundly. This effort consumed much of my life in 2009 and 2010 and I went all over the state of South Carolina. Sometimes I slept in my car because I did not have motel money. Sometimes I drove 200 miles, one way to attend a function, pass out handbills exposing

Barrett's record, and then drove 200 miles back home, all in the same day.

There were other people and other organizations making the same sort of sacrifices for good government. The 2010 victory of the *tea party* supported candidate for Governor of South Carolina, Nikki Haley, happened because lots of people worked long hours on the project and made sacrifices. I am very proud of the small part I played. However, it was never about me. Without the sacrifices of time and money by thousands of other citizens of this state, many of whom I have never met, we would not have achieved the victory.

Your purpose, as an organization, may be less ambitious than the defeat of every RINO Congressman in your state. Just make sure your purpose is very clear. Your purpose could be to elect constitutional conservatives as Republican Precinct Presidents in your county. [In some states they are called Precinct Chairmen.]

While it may not be absolutely necessary, a written goal, or formal *Mission Statement* can help you communicate your purpose clearly to all involved. Once you have a purpose, a goal, a project, a reason for existing as an organization, you can move to the next step. Here is an example of an excellent Mission Statement:

Spirit of Liberty, Inc.

Mission Statement

E Pluribus Unum!

Our mission is to celebrate and embrace the unity is the strength America draws from one culture, one language, and one nation under God today is truly *E Pluribus Unum!*

great strength, freedom and economic prosperity enjoyed by all Americans is firmly rooted in our one unique American history and cultural heritage.

Guided by divine providence, our founding fathers forged a republic whose guiding light and most fundamental principle they expressed in our national motto *E Pluribus Unum,* out of the many, one. It is oneness has made us great beyond all other civilizations have existed.

Thus Americans, descended from every corner of the earth, came to this continent to become one. *E Pluribus Unum.* One language, one legal system, one economic principle, one literature, and above all, one shared view of the rights and responsibilities endowed by our creator.

Our great strength, the marvel of the ages, derives from our unity under, one language, English, one system of cultural values, one legal system based upon the rule of law and upon our unique willingness to embrace all who are able to assimilate into our one nation under God indivisible. *E Pluribus Unum.*

Notice the name, Spirit of Liberty, Incorporated. The word Incorporated is very important. The word means the organization exists as a separate legal entity from its members who are individuals. This is an important legal protection will give members, and particularly leaders, of your group limited liability, protecting your money and property. In every state the process for creating a non-profit corporation is relatively easy and not very expensive. Chances are the leader of your tea party can do this without professional help, or perhaps one or more members of your group is a lawyer who will volunteer to do it for you.

Aside from limited liability, there are other uses and advantages to being incorporated as well. It is usually necessary to have some formal business structure in order to open bank accounts. It is also necessary before you may apply to the IRS for status as a non-profit organization pursuant to § 501 (c)(3) of the federal tax code.

Those on the political left are masters at getting the maximum legal benefits, funding, and organization in place for any project they undertake. Less than three weeks after the Occupy Wall Street protests started, I received the following e-mail message:

"Most protesters still can't define their goals beyond ending capitalism and making life more fair, which means they want other people's money. Meanwhile, donations of goods and cash pile up, with a reported $500,000 on deposit.

The cash marks an embarrassment for a movement supposedly railing against capitalism and wealth, especially now a radical group called the Alliance for Global Justice is legally sponsoring the protest. By lending its tax-exempt status - for a 7% cut! - The global justice group allows donors to deduct their contributions from federal taxes and gives its own board control over the money.

The alliance, based in Washington, is a hotbed of far left causes range from backing hunger strikes in California prisons to denouncing the CIA and oil companies. Its website says the group sponsors operations in the Gaza Strip, with Hamas, and boasts of an alliance with Anarchists Against the Wall, which contests Israel's security barrier in the West Bank."

The group suggests it has a relationship with Iran, supported the Sandinista revolution in Nicaragua and expresses solidarity with Venezuela's Hugo Chavez against the United States.

For the seven percent fee, it offers its tax-exempt status to "grassroots nonprofits" and provides payroll services, liability insurance, and prepares federal tax forms. It also offers *"activist training"* - which is like job training without an actual job.

Why should your local tea party group consider applying to the IRS for tax-exempt status? There is more to be gained than just the federal tax deduction members may claim for donations to the cause. Once you have the 501 (c)(3) status you will also be eligible for foundation grants. There actually are tax-exempt foundations are conservative not just the more famous ones on the left.

I recently attended a campaign school put on by a major national conservative organization. One of the things the lady presenting the seminar specifically mentioned was, her organization was willing to make financial grants to qualified local organizations - like *tea parties* - to promote political education and organization efforts. The major requirement is simply the organization receiving the money must qualify under Section 501 (c)(3) of the IRS code as a non-profit organization.

How is your *tea party* currently funded? Most of those I know, are funded by each member spending his or her own money on expenses; and, they are not getting any tax deduction for doing so either! When there are expenses for things other than personal travel and food, those expenses usually come out of the pocket of the local leaders. Most groups doing any fund raising at all are trying to sell a few books, CDs, or T-Shirts. I can tell you from years of experience such fund-raisers rarely break even and often require the leaders to buy a bunch of CDs or T-Shirts, most of which never get sold.

I would love for every *tea party* organization in America to sell this book. Candidly it is probably not going to make you or I a lot of money. My reason for suggesting you sell this book is because the information in this book will help you achieve your goal of saving our republic.

To raise serious money for your operations, consider becoming a non-profit corporation that qualifies for foundation grants pursuant to 26 USC § 501 (c)(3).

Get organized! You and fifteen friends have gotten together and agreed to work as a team, to accomplish a worthy purpose. It is time for you to be transformed from a bunch of like-minded individuals, into a team working together to accomplish your mutually agreed purpose. The simplest form of organization is to select a leader, identify all the steps necessary to have success, and assign each of those steps to one or more members who will accomplish them.

Larger groups, complex projects, and particularly, long term projects; are usually best accomplished with somewhat more formal organization. It is usually most convenient and efficient to operate with written by-laws, elected officers, and some sort of permanent legal structure.

Get trained! We are fortunate in my county there are several local attorneys who are very sympathetic to the *tea party* movement. One volunteered to host a training session on parliamentary procedure. We met around the conference table in his office, someone brought in Pizza and soft drinks, and the lawyer spent almost four hours teaching about a dozen of us the finer points of Parliamentary procedure. That education paid off nicely as we all attended the County GOP convention and then the State GOP convention where we put the training to good use.

Training and education should become part of the permanent activities of your organization. As you accomplish goals, you will find yourselves adopting new goals and working toward those. When you are more involved in the political process, you will learn there are seasons in politics just as there are seasons for sports or hunting game.

Read your state election laws and the local and state rules of the Republican Party where you live. You can find copies of these online. Some activities go on year round, recruiting, fund raisin, and education, are always necessary. Other things, precinct reorganization, or primary elections happen in some years, and not in other years. Customize your organization's projects to become as effective as possible at influencing the outcome of whatever activities are happening right now.

Earn Respect! Your organization is being watched by all your potential friends, as well as by your adversaries. The local news media is watching you. The success or failure of your projects will determine how respected your organization is within the larger community. You particularly want to have the respect of the local Republican Party, other conservative organizations, and the community where you reside.

There are no secrets and no shortcuts to earning respect. Work hard, organize efficiently, accomplish your goals, and, to the degree possible, show respect for other people and organizations. It is so much nicer to have others bragging on your successes, rather than having to defend and explain your failures.

Form Alliances! This is absolutely essential to your success. There is nothing at all wrong with an organization having a purpose is limited to one single issue. For example, the most important issue to your tea party might be preventing tax increases and reducing government spending. That is a fine goal and a sound conservative position. From time to time you will want to elect people to public office who share your views. Between elections, your tea party will want to influence legislation at the local, state, and national level to prevent tax and budget increases.

is where forming alliances with other conservative groups and organizations becomes crucial. In order to win an election you must have the votes of a majority of the voters who turn out on Election Day for your candidates. Not everyone in your community will see keeping taxes and government spending low as a number one priority the way you do. In order to have a winning campaign you must build a coalition including voters with other interests, as long as they do not disagree with your views on keeping taxes and spending low.

Folks who are most concerned with property rights are going to be natural supporters. That includes the National Association of Realtors, small business owners, the National Federation of Independent Businessmen, and probably most local bankers, not just the Taxpayers Association. Folks who are most concerned with protecting the right to keep and bear arms are also going to vote your way, so will many Veterans, truck drivers (especially owner/operators), as will your barber and your dentist.

Elections are won by turnout, not by opinions or poll numbers. Do not just assume all the folks concerned about property rights or gun rights will turn out and vote for your low tax candidates. Make a pro-active effort to reach out to them and communicate with them. They may not be coming to your anti-tax rallies, protests, and meetings. Therefore you need to go to meetings of Gun Owner's Rights organizations as well as shooting ranges and especially Gun Shows, to get out the word about your candidates.

Remember, elections are not won by the candidate who is smartest, the one who is right on the issues, or even the one who is doing the best in the polls. They are won by the candidate who gets the most supporters to actually turn out on Election Day!

One of the key sources of strength among our enemies on the far left is their amazing ability to form coalitions and alliances among folks who have very different interests.

What do homosexual activists; Black Baptist preachers, and thugs in the local labor union have in common? On the surface, you would think not much! The union goons are mainly interested in beating up workers who will not vote to unionize, or join an existing union. The homosexuals want to marry each other. The preacher wants to tell folks about Jesus. However, these three unlikely amigos will each be voting for the same candidate for Congress because the Democrat party and the communist party learned decades ago coalitions of folks with completely different interests can defeat Republicans by helping each other.

Certainly the primary purpose of your tea party organization may be limited to one issue like keeping taxes and government spending low. Just don't overlook folks in other organizations, including those whose purpose is a different issue. They will be your natural allies on Election Day.

Develop social contacts and personal relationships with the leaders of other organizations. Make sure there is good communications between the different organizations. You want to reduce government spending and keep down all taxes - period. Another organization does not want the government spending tax dollars to pay for abortions. Abortion may not be the number one issue of your tea party, but if you are comfortable adding abortion to a long list of things you do not want government dollars spent to pay for, you just picked up some very powerful allies on Election Day.

There are many fine conservative organizations around have been organized for years, have millions of members, and are very good at fund raising and public education. The NRA, founded in 1871 is a good example.

As conservatives, we are individuals. We do not see ourselves as part of a group. That strong independence makes us successful in business, and natural leaders in our communities, has also kept us from getting organized before we thought there was a crisis. We do not see ourselves as members of a race, part of a rigidly defined social class, or define ourselves by where our ancestors came from, in the manner most liberals do.

Most of my ancestors were Irish - five generations ago! Perhaps my Great Great Great Great Grandfather, who was with Washington's Army at Valley Forge, saw himself as an Irishman. Today it would be silly for me to go around telling people I am an Irish-American. I am just an American. Period. If I identify with any geographical area, I am also a Southerner.

As conservatives, the things important to us are our family, our Church, and then perhaps the profession we practice. Ask a conservative to describe himself and he will say, "*I am a truck driver.*" Or perhaps "*I am an attorney.*" Once in a while he may even say, "*I am a Methodist.*" Our rugged individualism tends to keep us from forming organizations to look out for our political interests the way the liberals do. It also keeps the tea parties, and other organizations we form, from entering into alliances with different organizations to create the massive coalitions needed to win elections, influence legislation and shape budgets between elections.

To protect our rights, our liberties, and our property we are going to have to get over the aversion to being well organized, and forming strong, powerful, coalitions with others who are also organized. This is one of the keys to protecting our rights and winning elections. The left already understands the power of this principle - form alliances - they work.

Once your tea party is organized, get out of your comfort zone. Go visit the NRA, Veterans organizations, churches other than your own, social organizations, join professional associations and fraternal organizations. When there is pending legislation, which will increase the federal budget, or raise the debt ceiling, and your US Congressman needs to get 5,000 telephone calls and e-mails - they are not all going to come from the 25 activists who come to your monthly tea party meeting.

Those 25 activists better know the importance of forming coalitions. Those 25 activists need to each influence 250 other folks in the property rights association, the pro-life groups, the NRA, veterans organizations, the local bar association, bankers association, Realtors association, Republican Women's Club, Chamber of Commerce, Lions Club, Masonic Lodge, Rotary, the Civil Air Patrol - or where ever you can influence folks to make those calls. You will have influence because they know you as a friend who has formed a personal relationship and who also cares about projects and charities important to them. This is the only workable formula for winning elections and influencing pending legislation.

Chapter Nine

No Third Party!

Political amateurs often make mistakes seasoned veterans would never consider. One such mistake is to dwell on what you believe should be, or what might have been, as opposed to what actually is. There is a fundamental fact about the political system in the United States of America for at least the last 200 years. We have a firmly entrenched two party system. The names of the parties have changed over time. Parties have been dissolved and replaced by different parties; and, most recently, the Democrat and Republican parties even switched philosophy between 1860 and 1980. By switching philosophy I mean the Republican Party, under Abe Lincoln in 1860 started out as the party of left wing ideas and big government. Remember Abe Lincoln and Karl Marx were contemporaries. Marx greatly admired Lincoln and wrote him a warm letter congratulating him on his re-election as president in 1864.

Conversely, during the *Reconstruction* era following the War Between the States, it was the Democrat Party that defended the constitution, free enterprise, and limited government, under the banner of *states rights*. Between 1860 and 1980 the philosophical positions of each of these two major parties had completely reversed.

None of this changes the fact, ours has been a two party system for more than 200 years. Many other countries do not have our tradition of two parties seeking to govern, and one or the other usually needing a majority to govern. Under our system, there is always a ruling party, with one other major party relegated to the status of the loyal opposition.

It is possible for one party to control the executive branch, the presidency, while the other party controls the legislative branch of government. Our Congress is a bicameral body, comprised of a

Senate and a House of Representatives. It is possible for one political party to control one house of Congress, while the other party controls the other house.

What is not possible under our system is government by more than two parties. Many parts of the world, most notably the British Commonwealth, have multi-party systems. This form of government is known as a Parliamentary system.

Under a Parliamentary system, it is common to have as many as five or more parties. Even though one or two of those parties may be dominant, the ruling party quite often holds less than a majority of the seats in the legislature and must form coalitions with minor parties to aggregate the support of a majority and be allowed to govern. Under such systems, radical parties focus on religion, as in Israel, or nationalism, as in much of Europe, may form coalition governments even if they are fourth or fifth place in elections.

This is because some party must have a coalition aggregates a majority of the seats in the elected Parliament. Under this system, the people do not elect the Prime Minister, the members of Parliament elect the Prime Minister. This is similar to the way the US House of Representatives chooses its Speaker. Under this system, the Queen of England, as the nominal head of state, will formally invite a leader of either the Labor, or the Conservative, party to *form a government*.

This invitation usually goes to the party leader whose party has won the most seats in the recent election. Assume, for example, the Labor Party has 45% of the seats in Parliament, and has been invited to form a government. Labor Party leader must now find another party with 6% or more of the seats in Parliament, who will be willing to form a coalition government with his party. It is not uncommon to see the party leader invited to form a government going to minor parties may have finished third, fourth, or even lower in the last election, as long as they can supply the 6% more seats he needs to have a majority coalition and form a government.

Forming a government, under this system, means the ability to appoint Cabinet Ministers and govern the country. It is common under these circumstances, to offer the leaders of the minor party in the coalition one, or more, Cabinet Ministries.

In countries with this Parliamentary form of government, it may be good strategy to make your appeal as broad as possible, in hopes of attracting a majority of the voters to your party in the hope you will not need to form a coalition with a minor party. Conversely, a minor party, organized around something regional, or radical, or religious, or what ever may elect a few seats even though they know ahead of time, they will never elect a majority of seats. The hope of such minor parties is, by having a few seats in Parliament, a major party with a plurality, but not a majority, of seats may need to court your party and entice you into a coalition forms the government and shares political power.

As you can see, while all this is very fascinating, to those of us who love politics or history; it is very different from our system here in the USA.

Basically, in a Parliamentary system, it is customary for party leaders to wheel and deal and form governing coalitions AFTER an election is over and the voters have spoken. In contrast, under our system, all the courting, and wheeling and dealing is done before the election by politicians and candidates making promises, and the voters make the final decision on election day.

There are advantages and disadvantages to each of these two very different systems of government. There have always been people who advocated the United States adopting some form of a Parliamentary government with its characteristic multiple party system, and deal making after elections are over.

That makes an interesting philosophical discussion, but has no place in this book on practical politics in the world as it actually exists here in the USA.

Why then have I digressed into a discussion of Parliamentary governments with multiple parties if is not possible here? The answer to question is very important to all the folks in the *tea party* movement. Your adversaries constantly complain the *tea party* folks are unwilling to compromise and therefore you impede progress. What you are really impeding is *business as usual*, and the only thing you are thwarting is their ability to spend our money - trillions of dollars of our money, and do it without our permission.

The opposition also raises the fallacious argument the *tea party* movement will somehow hurt the Republican party because it will alienate *independent* middle-of-the-road, undecided, voters who will be likely to be more comfortable with a less strictly constitutional position on some issue.

These arguments are disingenuous and based upon the incorrect premise our political system, like Parliamentary systems in Europe, consist of this third, or independent, party whose loyalty is necessary in order to form a governing coalition. is simply not true in the American political model with a two-party system.

There are indeed many people in America who consider themselves to be independent and do not necessarily always align themselves with either the Democrat, or the Republican Party. However, on Election Day, 95% of these independent minded people will, if they bother to vote, decide at least temporarily, to align with one, or the other, of the major parties.

It is very important to understand this for two reasons. On Election Day some of these independent voters, if they are dissatisfied with all choices, may simply decide not to vote. That is absolutely OK and your position on the issues should never be affected by what the folks who are not going to bother to vote anyway may think about things. Remember your real job is to lay out a clear vision of where you want to take America and give a lucid defense of your positions, including why those positions and policies are exactly right. In manner, you will attract *independent* voters to your position.

The left wing talking heads in the media, and in academia, want to accuse tea party activists of alienating these independent voters, by not being willing to compromise on positions, and go along to get along. In reality, lukewarm programs do not win over the undecided, making them adherents of our philosophy. Being willing to compromise and cut deals, abandoning principles for the *quid pro quo*, not only does not encourage undecided voters to move into our column. In many cases it actually turns them off because at best they see it as politics-as-usual, and at worst, as graft or corruption.

The beneficial role of the tea party is to become the conscience of the Republican Party and hold it true to its Platform and principles, no matter how hard the left wails against our intransigence.

Those who are new to politics, and who have never studied much US history, often raise the possibility of starting a new political party that will become the mythical *third party* of American politics. The reality is, we have always had lots of *minor parties*. The proponents of each of these *minor parties* would like to cast their *minor party* as the *Third Party*.

A real *Third Party* would elect Congressmen, Senators, and Governors, would be on the ballot in all fifty states, and would have at least some state and local elected officials all over the country. There has not been one of those since the Republicans in 1854. Even then, there was no three party system. The Whigs basically imploded just as the Republican Party sprang to life. The Republicans really started in 1854 as the Second Party (after the Democrats) and they won a fractured Presidential election in 1860, with a geographically limited base. Lincoln lost every Southern state. In Texas his name was not even on the ballot in 1860 and he did not get a single popular vote!

While we have had no true *Third Party* since the Republicans. There have been independent Presidential campaigns that ran a third candidate. We look at the results of several of these below. However, we must first notice an independent candidate for President causing an anomalous three-way race is not the same thing as an actual *Third Party*.

When we look at Theodore Roosevelt, Robert M. LaFollett, J. Strom Thurmond, George C. Wallace, H. Ross Perot, and Ralph Nader, in each case, we see a cult of personality, rather than any actual third political party.

There have also been ideological minor parties all through our history. There were the Know Nothings, the Anti-Masonic Party, the Prohibition Party, the Socialist, Socialist Labor, Socialist Workers, Farm Labor, Conservative, Constitution, American, American Independent, Green, Black Panther, States Rights, Populist, Progressive, Peace & Freedom, Reform, Communist, La Raza Unita (English translation: "The Race United"), and Libertarian; to mention a few of the many.

A few of these political parties were on the ballot for decades. Some were able to appear on the ballot in most states. Some were effective in impacting statewide elections in geographical regions. Some of them have even managed to elect a few people to local office upon occasion. In some cases disgruntled elected officials have switched from Republican to Libertarian, but *none* of those was ever re-elected as a Libertarian. Former Governors J. Strom Thurmond, George Wallace, and Lester Maddox, were elected as Democrats and later ran for president on minor parties; none won election on the minor party ticket.

J. Strom Thurmond, of South Carolina has the distinction of being the only person in history to ever win a state wide election as a Republican, a Democrat, a States Rights Party candidate*, and on a Write-In.

*Thurmond carried the state of South Carolina in the 1948 Presidential election but was not elected President.

In 1912 former President Theodore Roosevelt, denied re-nomination as a Republican, launched his independent bid under the banner of the *Progressive Party*, popularly known as the *Bull Moose Party*. Teddy Roosevelt received 4.1 million popular votes to Republican William Howard Taft's 3.5 million votes. Roosevelt also garnered 88 electoral votes. The result was the election of Democrat Woodrow Wilson.

In 1948 Southern Democrats were very unhappy with President Harry Truman because Truman ordered the racial integration of the US Armed Forces and the national Democrat party adopted an unpopular civil rights plank in the 1948 national party platform. South Carolina Governor J. Strom Thurmond ran for president as a *States Rights Democrat*, popularly known as a *Dixiecrat*. Thurmond received 39 electoral votes.

The real effect of the Thurmond candidacy was to keep Southern Democrats who were unhappy with Harry Truman and the national Democrat Party, from voting Republican for Thomas Dewey. Clearly the Thurmond candidacy had exactly two effects; first, it insured Southern Democrats deserting Truman did not gravitate to the Republican Party, which would have cost Truman the election. Second, the Thurmond candidacy gave Southerners an excuse not to desert the Democrat Party as they would later do in response to Reagan's 1980 appeal to become 'Reagan' Democrats.

In 1968 Alabama's Democrat Governor, George C. Wallace, formed the *American Party* and entered the presidential election opposing Democrat Hubert H. Humphrey and Republican Richard Nixon. Wallace carried almost 10 million popular votes, or 13% for 45 electoral votes. Once again, the *third party* did not win and the major effect of the Wallace campaign was to forestall for another 12 years, the inevitable realignment of the South from the Democrat Party to the Republican Party that finally took place in 1980. That year Ronald Reagan made it OK to be a *"Reagan Democrat"* in the South. We now have second-generation Reagan Democrats in the South who have never voted for anything but a Republican for president in their lives. Their children and grandchildren will never go back to the Democrat Party.

In 1992 incumbent President George H. W. Bush went into his re-election campaign with a 90% public approval rating following our victory in the 100 hour long first Gulf War. Bush appeared to be cruising toward an easy re-election if not to a landslide. Major, respected, Democrat Party heavyweights like Mass. Senator Edward Kennedy and New York Governor Mario Coumo, decided to stay out of the Democrat Party primaries year.

The conventional wisdom was that 1992 was going to be a Republican landslide and losing an election to George H. W. Bush, would not be good for the career of up and coming Democrat contenders. The candidates who filed for the Democrat primaries were seen as second-string politicians who were just going through the motions, or positioning themselves for the future.

All the conventional wisdom was based upon a normal election between incumbent Republican President George H. W. Bush, and the eventual Democrat nominee, in a traditional two-man race.

Texas businessman H. Ross Perot made millions of dollars, mostly by selling computers to the Social Security Administration, and other government agencies. Perot was a little man with a huge ego. While earning his millions, Perot had also developed an intense dislike for the President of the United States, George H. W. Bush that bordered on a vendetta.

Perot formed the *Reform Party* which was largely self funded with his personal millions. He managed to get on the ballot in all 50 states. Because the voters were impressed with his label as a no nonsense businessman, Perot was initially taken seriously by a major segment of our electorate, actually polling second in several states.

Then Perot withdrew from the race in late summer, claiming, among other things President George H. W. Bush had used the CIA to disrupt his daughter's wedding! Then Perot got back into the race even though he was no longer polling double digit support, He was able to keep going because his *Reform Party* was largely funded with his personal millions. The left leaning mainstream media also fell all over themselves to build up someone who was drawing votes away from President Bush.

On Election Day, Perot did not win a single electoral vote and carried only about 9% of the popular vote. However, almost all of the Perot votes came from people who would otherwise have voted for Bush the Republican. The result of the Perot candidacy was the election of Democrat Bill Clinton to the presidency with less than a majority of the popular vote. Had there been no Perot candidacy; there would have been no Clinton presidency! Period.

The last example we need to look at is the Presidential Election in 2000. Once again, the outcome was decided by just a hand full of votes for a minor party candidate in just one state - Florida. Most of you remember both the popular vote and the electoral vote were very close between Republican George W. Bush, and Democrat Al Gore.

The outcome of the election turned on votes cast in the state of Florida. The vote in Florida was so close there were recounts conducted in several populous counties. In the end, both sides claimed victory, both sides filed lawsuits, and the resulting cases went all the way to the US Supreme Court. By the narrowest of margins, only 537 popular votes, Bush, the Republican was determined to be the winner of the Florida election, and therefore became the President of the United States.

Goofball anti-business lawyer, and perennial minor candidate for office, Ralph Nader ran the third of his quixotic races for President in 2000 as the candidate of the far left *Green Party*.

Nationally Nader made very little difference and he got just over 2 million popular votes and no electoral votes. Why then was Ralph Nader crucial to the George W. Bush victory in 2,000? The answer was the 97,421 popular votes Ralph Nader received in Florida, way more than the 537 vote margin of Bush over Gore. It does not take the proverbial Rocket Scientist to see that with Nader off the Florida ballot, his far left supporters would have either voted for Democrat Al Gore, or stayed home. It is inconceivable any serious portion of the Ralph Nader votes would have gone to George W. Bush.

Clearly in 1992 H. Ross Perot, running as a conservative businessman had caused the defeat of George H. W. Bush in his campaign for re-election. Just as clearly, in 2000 Bush's son had been *elected* president because radical loon Ralph Nader, running on the far left *Green Party*, siphoned off almost 100,000 votes from Democrat Al Gore in the critical state of Florida.

There is a lesson here for any of the tea party activists who may have considered, or advocated, the formation of a minor political party. One they hope could grow into the proverbial, but elusive, *Third Party*. The clear evidence is minor parties never rise to the level of becoming a true and lasting *Third Party,* even if they occasionally come in third place in a presidential election.

The other clear fact about such parties is, more often than not, they are actually responsible for the election of the major party candidate most different from them. To put it another way, conservative minor parties [T. Roosevelt, Thurmond, Wallace, Perot] have all helped elect Democrats much more liberal than the Republican candidate they opposed. Meanwhile, minor candidates on the left [Ralph Nader] actually made possible the election of a man running as a conservative Republican, George W. Bush.

Minor parties always take votes away from the major party candidate whose philosophy is most close to their own, with the result of helping elect the major party candidate whose philosophy and platform are least like their own.

A conservative, tea party oriented, minor party next year would draw all of its votes from the Republican nominee and the result would be to make it more likely Mr. Obama would be re-elected, not less likely.

Most of the folks in the tea party movement are smart enough to understand these things and there has been very little talk of the tea party movement forming any Tea Party political party.

Finally, I actually would like to see another minor party on the general election ballot in 2012, at least in the state of Florida. I hope to see the **United Negro Homosexual Trial-Lawyer's Muslim Green Illegal Alien Socialist Union Party** on the ballot, to once more get all those votes went to Ralph Nader in 2000. In fact, they can run Ralph Nader again, with either Maxine Waters, or, Barney Frank for vice President.

is to say, the Obama folks should have to worry about a third party nightmare scenario, not the constitutional conservatives in our *tea party* movement.

Chapter Ten

Moving From Protest, To Activist

The tea party movement sprang so dramatically on the scene in 2009 was primarily a protest movement. More properly, it was a series of hundreds of protests large and small, all over America. There was no one incident sparked the movement; no one leader who called it forth, and no one issue provoked its eruption

The closest thing to a unifying theme was, government has gotten too large, too expensive, too intrusive into our lives and, above all, too unresponsive to and out of touch with us. There was no Howard Jarvis to lead these protestors, but his refrain of *"I am mad as hell and not going to take it anymore!"* was being heard loud and clear.

These protestors were a class of people too refined to riot but too angry to quietly write letters to Congressmen and newspaper editors any longer. They respected the law. They respected private property. They were guided by a strong sense of morality and knew the difference between right and wrong. Others were not goading these protestors into action. They were not in the street to loot, plunder, rape or pillage the property of others. The tea party, in contrast to riots and protests of the left, was driven into the public square by righteous indignation over their own property being looted. Not only was the government failing to protect their rights and property, in many cases, it was the government itself was looting its most loyal and productive citizens.

The tea party movement was not an organized army marching in lockstep and wearing fancy uniforms. They were more of a rag-tag militia, undisciplined, disorganized, and poorly led. Our republic was born in a bloody baptism of fire. Untrained militia had defeated larger armies of seasoned professionals. The members of the modern *tea party* movement were the descendants of those Patriots of 1776. In a very real sense the *tea party* movement of 2009 reflected this heritage in more ways than just waving rattlesnake flags reading *"Don't tread on me."*

This was a true insurgency rising from the bottom up. These were ordinary Americans driven by frustration almost to the brink of despair. They had been betrayed by the very institutions, which were supposed to be the fabric of our civilization.

The citadels of academia had long ago fallen to radicals working tirelessly to undermine free enterprise. The American Revolution had been first preached from the pulpits of America's Churches. The modern Church has shied away from taking moral stands. Pastors, Priests, and Rabbi's failed to decry the injustice of forced wealth redistribution. Means of mass communications, radio, TV and print media, were more properly the propaganda arms of the state, than places to obtain unbiased and accurate information.

Above all, the political process which is supposed to make our representative government the watchdog of our liberties had been subverted by the corrupting influences of big money, where vocal special interests wield power disproportionate to their numbers.

The *tea party* movement was millions of people who finally got fed up with all these trends and decided to pour, not into the streets as leftists would, but onto Courthouse squares and other public property all over America. They braved freezing rain in February and blistering heat in July, to tell their neighbors it was time to take our country back from the far left. Enough is enough, this country belongs to the people who built it and we are evicting the leeches have been squatting here!

The *tea party* movement was more remarkable because there was not any one socio-economic group participating. There were not just women in our numbers but children too. The tea party movement is a family oriented activity. This was not a movement for only black people, or only white people. The local tea party tended to look a lot like the local population. There were Jews, Catholics, Protestants and just about every religious persuasion imaginable, with the notable exception of Moslems. This was not a movement of the downtrodden and poverty stricken, nor was it the movement of the wealthy elite. Every economic strata of society came together for the common cause of shrugging off the yoke of an unresponsive government, bloated at every level.

With a few exceptions, most of the people making speeches at these gatherings were not political leaders or elected officials. Many of them were not well educated and certainly not experienced public speakers. They were ordinary, middle-class, Americans *speaking from the heart* to their neighbors.

What they lacked in eloquence or sophistication was more than compensated by the passion, sincerity, truth, and fairness of the message being delivered. The message, delivered in a hundred different ways, always expressed in some form, our government has grown too big, our tax burden is too high, and the institutions are supposed to serve and protect our interests have been subverted by socialists and communists. The simple call to action was *"It is time to take back our America!"*

I remember reading a hand-lettered sign in Washington, D.C. September 12, 2009. It read simply, *"IF THE FIRST AMENDMENT DOES NOT WORK TRY THE SECOND!"*

Fortunately for America, the First Amendment did work - it worked beautifully. The media ridiculed the *tea partiers*, but their neighbors noticed them. The news organizations understated the numbers present at protests, but your neighbors were in those gatherings and saw the truth.

If 2009 was the year of the protest, 2010 could be characterized as the year of the activist. Millions of Americans protesting bloated government did not go unnoticed. They certainly caught the attention of those of us who have been fighting all these same issues for fifty years. It was almost as if someone said *"there is a whole bunch of sweet fruit growing wild by the side of the road and all you have to do is pick it."*

Those of us who have been the movement conservatives since the Goldwater days did not start the *tea party* movement, nor were we its leaders. As noted earlier, in spite of all the claimants and organizations which have rushed forward to claim authorship of this movement, or offer it leadership, no one person or group may legitimately claim responsibility for the 2009 year of protests. In every sense they were truly spontaneous. This is absolutely a case of the *100th Monkey Syndrome* manifesting itself.

By early 2010 as the modern tea party movement celebrated its first birthday the staging of mass protests began to die out as spontaneously as it had sprang from the earth. Participants at multiple *tea party* protests began to exchange contact information. Strong personalities, people who have been successful in business, stepped forward to suggest meetings instead of protests.

The *Tea Party* moved indoors. It was no longer on the grounds of the Statehouse, or in the County Square, with homemade signs and Gadsden rattlesnake flags. The *tea party* movement was now meeting in people's living rooms, in public restaurants, in public libraries, on college campuses, and even in bars. It was almost as if this movement had come full circle, and, after 238 years found itself once more in the great room of Boston's famous *Green Dragon Tavern*.

During the first great year of protest, we looked for dates with historic, or political, significance and planned protests on Washington's Birthday, April 15th, Flag Day on June 14th, the 4th of July, on September 17th we remembered the adoption of the constitution, and on December 15th the ratification of the Bill of Rights.

The following year *tea party* groups were more likely to be meeting in advance of significant dates to plan action ahead. The dates shifted from holidays, and historic remembrances. The dates selected in 2010 were much more likely to be the last day to register and vote before an election, the date on which Republican Party precinct reorganizations were accomplished, the date of county and state Republican conventions, and the dates of Republican Party county and state Executive Committee meetings. Almost imperceptibly the tea party movement underwent a metamorphosis, from a protest movement, to an activist movement. Tea party activists were now educating themselves on how the political process works.

They began to understand the country did not get into an economic, moral, and political mess overnight when Mr. Obama won an election. The rot had grown within the republic for decades.

In part, the rot had grown because these very *tea party* participants, for the most part, had neglected citizenship and community service. Over the course of those same decades the community activists on the far left had been well organized and working busy as little beavers.

For the first time, as more tea party participants began to understand how our political institutions and processes actually work, it dawned on them, they had more than a little guilt for how bad things have gotten in all the years they were making a living, going to Church, playing football, and generally enjoying life without a care or responsibility for who was making the millions of economic and political decisions that affect their daily lives in countless ways.

It is said no Christian has more zeal than a new convert and no crusader against drinking or smoking has quite the rabid fervency of someone who has himself recently renounced such addictions. In like manner, among the most fervent of constitutional conservative activists are the participants of the *tea party* movement. What they lacked in understanding, maturity, or judgment, was to be made up for with zeal, ambition, hard work, and diligently applying one's self to master the operations of our political system. At times, it was a steep learning curve.

The demagogues and uneducated among the *tea party* movement continued to cynically castigate the political system as unfair and unduly influenced by corruption, conspiracy, or both. The more honest and intelligent among the *tea party* ranks recognize the system was not fundamentally flawed, as much as they themselves were culpable for having failed to participate and protect their own rights and interests.

A word about cynics and conspiracy buffs is in order. The enemies of the *tea party* movement tried, unsuccessfully to portray the movement as racist, and failed largely because the movement not only is not racist, it vigorously rejects racism. What happened was millions of Americans protested. They did not protest Mr. Obama's race; they protested *his* racism!

The tea party movement would have grown quicker and earned more legitimate political power and respect if it had been as vigorous in weeding out and socially ostracizing conspiracy nuts as it had been in rejecting racists.

The use of the word *nigger* was abhorrent and prohibited as it is in the community at large. Sadly, nobody confronted and ostracized the people who made the much more unacceptable claim the United States Government carried out the attacks on 9/11/2001 as part of some "*false flag*" operation to blame the adherents of Islam. Far too few people were willing to tell the blame America first crowd "*you are not welcome here, go away!*"

There are certainly quite legitimate complaints, which may be raised about a federal agency like FEMA. We can start with the unconstitutionality of attempting to respond to disasters with the resources of the federal government. Aside from being unconstitutional, it has also been ineffective, corrupt, wasteful, mismanaged, politicized, incompetent, and has generally thrown away billions of dollars with both hands. These deficiencies are well known and easily documented I have first hand experience with the response to the human tragedy caused by hurricanes Katrina and Rita along the Gulf coast in Louisiana and Mississippi.

Along with another Veterans of Foreign Wars State Chaplain, I helped raise tens of thousands of dollars for hurricane relief, a truckload of supplies, and went to the Mississippi Gulf coast and stayed almost two weeks delivering money, water, food and other relief supplies. We worked 14 hour days, and I slept in a cot on the dance floor inside the VFW Post Home in Gulfport, which had become a temporary center for relief supplies. Once we gave away our food, water and money, we stayed. We helped unload trucks, 18-wheelers not pickups, with donated relief supplies from individuals, churches, VFW Posts and private businesses.

The trucks came from all over the United States. Local leaders in the VFW Post made sure the goods went to people who needed them. They also made sure nothing was wasted and nothing went to anyone trying to commit fraud to get something for nothing. To put it bluntly, the same cannot be said of the billions of dollars that went through FEMA, to the politically connected and those who knew how to milk the government system for "*benefits and entitlements.*"

I mention this to tell you I have intimate, personal, first-hand, knowledge of how FEMA responded to hurricanes Katrina and Rita. I mention FEMA as a government program that justifies a lot of criticism. However, the *tea party* movement has been remiss in not confronting, and rejecting the nutty conspiracy theorists who claim FEMA is constructing concentration camps for Americans.

Shortly after Mr. Obama was elected I received a number of e-mails telling me FEMA was establishing a national network of concentration camps. They had supposedly already Pre-selected those of us to be rounded up. Color-coded markers on a mailbox or fence post designated our homes. If your home was designated with a red marker, you and your family were to be killed immediately. Those with blue markers would be imprisoned for life, and those with yellow markers would be sent to re-education camps but eventually released.

The first few times I saw this, I shrugged it off as the work of nutcase conspiracists in tinfoil hats. Then two things changed my mind. First, I got a call from a respected member of the legislature asking my opinion of these e-mails? Evidently he was getting them too and did not simply dismiss it outright.

Next, a few days later I took my dog for a walk through the neighborhood. I had forgotten conspiracy theories about concentration camps. Then, I saw them! There really were color-coded reflective stickers marking houses in my neighborhood! They really were red, blue and yellow. My own house had a blue sticker. That was too much of a coincidence. I now had to investigate this and get to the bottom of it.

I started by visiting the local Postmaster, showing him the sticker I removed from my own mailbox post, and asking him to explain how they helped with mail delivery? The Postmaster assured me he knew nothing about any of this, had never seen one of these stickers and they had nothing to do with mail delivery. Was he part of some federal cover up?

My next stop was a friend in the Sheriff's Department who assured me it had nothing to do with law enforcement and he had never seen any of the stickers before. At the time I held a senior position in the South Carolina State Guard and nobody there knew anything about it either. My friend who worked for the TSA as a baggage handler knew nothing either. Nor did the County Chairman of the Republican Party, or the Master of my Masonic Lodge. My attorney, my insurance man, my mechanic, and even my barber were just as mystified as I was and had never seen the reflective blue plastic disk.

Finally, I called the office of the local newspaper editor. The person answering the phone at the newspaper transferred my call to the Circulation Department. I was a bit miffed at being directed to the Circulation Department rather than the Editorial Desk. In response to the polite question from the fellow in circulation, I explained I needed editorial because I was investigating these color-coded disks all over my neighborhood.

The fellow in circulation replied, " *is why they transferred your call to Me.*" he explained "*You see, we put the red ones on houses that subscribe to the newspaper every day. The blue ones go on houses that only subscribe to the Sunday paper, and the yellow ones, are for the folks who subscribe to the week day edition but not the Sunday paper.*"

The mystery was solved. There was no conspiracy to put my family and I into a concentration camp. We were merely marked so the paper delivery boy knew, even in the pre-dawn darkness, to deliver a Sunday paper at our humble abode!

Some of these conspiracy believers may be sincere; some of the theories appear to have at least some merit, as with the strange reflective disks used by the paper delivery boy. Many of these theories, particularly about 9/11 are planted to intentionally discredit and confuse the *tea party* movement, as well as to discredit it to respectable political activists who should be natural allies.

In spite of mistakes, growing pains, and having a lot of amateurs working on a very steep learning curve, the *tea party* movement overcame its weaknesses, managed to pull together as an effective political force that continues to grow in power and professionalism every day. The *tea party* movement gave the Republican conservatives some amazing and unexpected primary upsets in 2010. The pundits all chimed in the tea party could not possibly win elections. The lamestream media as Sarah Palin has dubbed it, lamented the fact the Republican Party had been hijacked by radicals and was saddled with far-right nominees who were unelectable.

We all know those predictions turned out to be about as accurate as most of the rest of the garbage spouted by the lamestream media over the last couple of decades. In reality 2010 was a conservative landslide and the *tea party* endorsement had been required to win elections in district after district, all over America!

We even picked up some long shot winners in US Senate races. All the media, and the pundits of the left in academia could do was claim the GOP would have done even better in US Senate races if they had not embraced the *tea party* nominees. The American people see through these liberal diatribes. To put it bluntly, the political left in this country has a lot of chicken manure in the chicken salad they are trying to sell and the voters know it.

Chapter XI

Tax Equity Act!

The founding fathers envisioned the federal government would be funded almost entirely on indirect taxes; duties, imposts, and excises. Duties and imposts, also known as tariffs, are taxes on goods imported from foreign countries. Excises are taxes on a license or privilege, usually a license to manufacture something like alcohol or firearms. Excises also include the privilege of doing business as a corporation. All of these are a class of taxes known as indirect taxes, which must be uniform throughout the United States according to the US constitution.

Tariffs did indeed raise revenue. However, there was also a policy goal involved in levying tariffs on imports. It was a protectionist measure. The tariff, or tax, on imported goods served to make those goods more expensive than similar goods manufactured in the United States, thus protecting domestic manufacturers from foreign competition.

Tariffs also allowed for the transfer of wealth from the southern part of the United States to the northern part. This use of Tariff laws was the primary cause of the War Between the States - not slavery. How did the Tariff transfer wealth from South to north? Southern planters had great wealth but much of it was in the form of cotton not cash money. Commerce with England, and to a lesser extent other countries, often consisted in bartering southern cotton for English manufactured goods. These English manufactured goods were both cheaper, and of better quality than similar goods manufactured in the North.

The purpose of Tariff laws was to accomplish two things. First, it raised most of the money to operate the federal government from Southern states with the north sharing in very little of the tax burden. This was because the South was very dependent upon international commerce, selling cotton abroad, and importing manufactured goods not made in the South. In contrast, the north sold almost all of its manufactured goods domestically and had almost no export business. Northerners also bought their own manufactured goods and imported very few goods from England. Thus the Tariff fell disproportionately upon the South. Under this system, Yankees paid almost no federal taxes while Southerners carried most of the load.

The other effect was to force Southerners to buy Yankee manufactured goods rather than importing such goods from England. The Tariff of 1860 was adopted after seven states seceded and control of the US Senate passed from the Democrat to the Republican Party. Tariffs were increased as much as 70%. The law was very popular in the north, but, understandably unpopular in the South as well as in England where it dried up export markets to the US, hurting English manufacturers.

The well known novelist Charles Dickens correctly wrote on December 28, 1861

"If it be not slavery, where lies the partition of the interests that has led at last to actual separation of the Southern from the Northern States? ...Every year, for some years back, this or Southern state had declared it would submit to this extortion only while it had not the strength for resistance. With the election of Lincoln and an exclusive Northern party taking over the federal government, the time for withdrawal had arrived ... The conflict is between semi-independent communities [in which] every feeling and interest [in the South] calls for political partition, and every pocket interest [in the North] calls for union ... So the case stands, and under all the passion of the parties and the cries of battle lie the two chief moving causes of the struggle. Union means so many millions a year lost to the South; secession means the loss of the same millions to the North. The love of money is the root of this, as of many other evils... [T]he quarrel between the North and South is, as it stands, solely a fiscal quarrel."

Robert Barnwell Rhett of South Carolina, a delegate to the Secession Convention of December 1860, helped draft the Confederate constitution, and was later elected to the Confederate Congress. On December 25, 1860 he wrote:

"And so with the Southern States, towards the Northern States, in the vital matter of taxation. They are in a minority in Congress. Their representation in Congress, is useless to protect

them against unjust taxation; and they are taxed by the people of the North for their benefit, exactly as the people of Great Britain taxed our ancestors in the British parliament for their benefit. For the last forty years, the taxes laid by the Congress of the United States have been laid with a view of subserving the interests of the North. The people of the South have been taxed by duties on imports, not for revenue, but for an object inconsistent with revenue— to promote, by prohibitions, Northern interests in the productions of their mines and manufactures."

Both the English, and Southern Democrats in the United States, were advocates of low tariffs and free trade. Northern Republicans did not merely disagree, they understood without the protection of high tariffs the north could not compete economically. The livelihood of northern industrialists and craftsmen alike was threatened by the prospect of a free South engaged in free trade with the rest of the world. If the port city of Charleston, South Carolina, was allowed to thrive as a low tariff point of entry, New York and Philadelphia would die on the vine. Charleston would become the one great economic gateway to the North American continent. Charleston would be closely followed by Mobile, New Orleans, and Galveston. Free trade, not slavery, was the scenario Mr. Lincoln was willing to go to war to prevent.

Mr. Lincoln's long, bloody, war to destroy the constitution and impose hegemony of northern bankers and industrialists upon the ruins of our constitutional republic would be enormously expensive. To pay for this war Lincoln resorted to two more unconstitutional schemes.

One of those was counterfeiting large sums of so called money, in violation of Article I Sections 8 and 10 of the Constitution, and of the Tenth Amendment. These counterfeits were known as Greenbacks. I will detail in the next chapter on currency reform how they defrauded the men who supplied war materials to the Union army during the war, then enriched foreign speculators and central banks after the war.

The other socialist scheme devised by Mr. Lincoln and his Republican Party to fund the War of Northern Aggression was the first income tax.

We touched earlier on the constitutional provision in Article I, Section 8, requiring all indirect taxes to be uniform. The constitution also required all direct taxes to be apportioned among the states according to their respective populations. Thus indirect taxes are to be uniform, and direct taxes are to be apportioned according to population.

I state these two great constitutional rules in the present tense for a reason, the United States Supreme Court has upheld them consistently, and they are still the law of the land today. In 1895 a constitutional challenge to the federal income tax reached the Supreme Court in the cases of *Charles Pollock v. Farmers Loan & Trust Company*, 157 U.S. 429 (1895) and 158 U.S. 601 (1895.) I say cases, because the case was re-heard before the US Supreme Court and there are actually two *Pollock Cases*.

In a 5-4 decision a majority of the Court overturned the 1895 income tax because it was an unapportioned direct tax, in violation of the clear provisions of the US constitution.

Over the next 18 years there were numerous parties of the left advocating Karl Marx's heavy, progressive, or graduated, income tax, as found in the Communist Manifesto. In 1913 the Sixteenth Amendment to the US constitution was adopted. Once again, in 1913 Congress imposed an Income Tax on Americans. Once again constitutional challenges to this law were raised. To resolve those legal challenges, the case went to the US Supreme Court. This time, it was *Frank R. Brushaber v. Union Pacific Railroad Company*, 240 U.S. 1, decided January 24, 1916.

Mr. Chief Justice White delivered the majority opinion of the court. He said, in relevant part, *"The various propositions are so intermingled as to cause it to be difficult to classify them. We are of opinion, however, the confusion is not inherent, but rather arises from the conclusion the 16th Amendment provides for a hitherto unknown power of taxation; is, a power to levy an income tax which, although direct, should not be subject to the regulation of apportionment applicable to all other direct taxes. And the far-reaching effect of this **erroneous assumption** (emphasis supplied) will be made clear by generalizing the many contentions advanced in argument to support it, as follows:"* He then went on to enumerate four provisions that violated the rule of apportionment.

Apologists for the Marxist income tax of 1913 have claimed the 16th Amendment to the US constitution removed the need for apportionment of any direct tax, among the states based upon population. The Supreme Court said in _Brushaber_, this was an "_erroneous assumption._" All income taxes are indirect taxes.

The opinion of the Court in _Brushaber_ continued "_But it clearly results the proposition and the contentions under it, if acceded to, would cause one provision of the Constitution to destroy another; is, they would result in bringing the provisions of the Amendment exempting a direct tax from apportionment into irreconcilable conflict with the general requirement all direct taxes be apportioned. Moreover, the tax authorized by the Amendment, being direct, would not come under the rule of uniformity applicable under the Constitution to other than direct taxes, and thus it would come to pass the result of the Amendment would be to authorize a particular direct tax not subject either to apportionment or to the rule of geographical uniformity, thus giving power to impose a different tax in one state or states than was levied in another state or states. This result, instead of simplifying the situation and making clear the limitations on the taxing power, which obviously the Amendment must have been intended to accomplish, would create radical and destructive changes in our constitutional system and multiply confusion._

These are not my words; they are the decision of the United States Supreme Court in _Brushaber_, which has never been overturned!

Our current federal income tax law is derived from this 1913 statute, as revised and amended many times. The original Act was only 10 pages long and imposed a modest tax of 2% on the income of individuals over $3,000 [$4,000 for married couples.] There were major revisions of the Tax Code in 1939, 1954, and again in 1987 with the Reagan era reforms. The King James Version of the Holy Bible has 783,137 words in it. Our current federal income tax law is over 7.8 million words; about ten times the size of the King James Bible. To which, you may add twenty volumes of regulations, according to the U.S. Government Printing Office, totaling another 13,458 pages. Added to these are literally hundreds of volumes of the reported cases rendered by the U.S. Tax Court, all of which, under the legal doctrine of _stare decisis_, are supposed to guide and inform your understanding of our current law.

It is a cliché among authors who have just summarized a complex subject to say *"I could write a book about it."* In fact, I have written several books on the subject since 1978.

How did a simple ten-page law in 1913 get transformed into the monstrosity we have just described? The surprising answer is something many Americans do not understand about our system of tax laws. It is debatable whether the purpose of our tax laws was ever entirely for the purpose of actually raising revenue. The goal of the Honorable members of the House Ways and Means Committee writing our federal income tax laws has been, not raising revenue, but to control economic activity. Allow me to illustrate the point with a true story here in South Carolina just a few years ago.

The citizens of the Upstate of South Carolina - the same folks who turned out 10,000 people for a tea party protest in 2009 - are very conservative. We sent Jim DeMint to Washington, D.C. to represent us as our Congressman. Former Rep. Bob Inglis followed him in office.

Bob is a tall, skinny, fellow with an unkempt crew-cut hairdo and a boyish grin. Before becoming a politician, Bob was a real estate lawyer, and he is reasonably bright, likeable, and an interesting fellow. He started his political career as a somewhat conservative middle-of-the-road sort of Republican. Somewhere along the way the years of living in the artificial environment in foggy bottom on the Potomac, convinced Bob the world faces a very serious crisis involving global warming, or climate change, and it is caused by human activity.

Bob worried till he developed a solution to this non-existent problem. His brilliant strategy is to replace all the cars on the road run on gasoline with a different kind of cars that will run on hydrogen gas as a fuel. To his credit, Bob loved to hold town hall meetings, often at a restaurant called Tommy's Ham House. In his Town Hall meetings, Bob would hold forth on his favorite subject, hydrogen powered cars, and explain to all who would listen, why hydrogen fueled cars must eventually replace our gasoline-powered cars.

We would explain to Congressman Bob Inglis that gasoline, which was selling for $1.65 a gallon at the time, was the most economical way to power motor vehicles, followed closely by diesel. Bob calmly explained to us how burning hydrocarbons made carbon dioxide, while burning pure hydrogen gas would leave only pure water vapor. The Congressman said he was working to get the price of gasoline up to around $5 to $7 per gallon like parts of Europe so we would stop using so much gasoline! He knew these so-called *alternative* fuels would not be economically feasible unless gasoline was selling at around $7 per gallon. He also knew people are going to buy what ever is the cheapest, not what the politically correct crowd happens to favor at the moment. The only way to cram this stuff down our throats is to make gasoline so expensive the new *alternatives* actually become cheaper.

Are you beginning to see why Bob Inglis is now a *former* Congressman? He clearly does not understand the recent volcanic eruption in Iceland spewed hundreds of times more carbon dioxide into the atmosphere in just a few months than all the activities of mankind upon the earth since the birth of Christ.

At one Town Hall meeting in 2009 I carefully explained to the Congressman just why hydrogen gas is not technologically feasible as an auto fuel. Unlike the former Congressman, I actually have some background and training in the industrial uses of hydrogen. I once worked for the *Linde Gas Division* of the *Union Carbide Corporation* in their chemical plant at Texas City, Texas.

My job there was to operate a compressor the size of the average middle class home, and fill hundreds of heavy metal cylinders with hydrogen gas compressed to over 2,400 pounds of pressure per square inch. If the brass valve gets knocked off one of these heavy steel cylinders, it becomes an unguided missile capable of flying through cinder block walls and killing anyone in its trajectory.

I explained to Congressman Bob Inglis, there was only one other way to use hydrogen as a fuel. When hydrogen gas is compressed to several hundred PSI and simultaneously cooled to -423.17 degrees below zero Fahrenheit, it becomes a liquid consisting of 99.79% parahydrogen and 0.21% orthohydrogen. [In parahydrogen, the two protons in the atomic nucleus spin in the same direction, while with orthohydrogen they spin in opposite directions.]

I also explained to the Congressman burning hydrogen in pure oxygen indeed results in harmless water vapor as a byproduct. However, burning hydrogen in the presence of nitrogen produces some very nasty toxic chemicals. Nitrogen is the main component of air being 78.09% of the mixture in dry air. To have his emissions free automobile fuel, Bob would need to burn pure oxygen, not ordinary air, in his automobile. With oxygen you once again have the options of heavy, and dangerous, compressed gas cylinders. The largest size commonly used is the K size, which is 9.25" in diameter, 60' tall (including a 5-inch valve) and holds 49.9 cubic feet of gas. These things weigh 134 pounds each when they are empty.

Again, there is the option of compressing and cooling oxygen until it becomes a pale blue liquid that will boil at -297.33 degrees below zero Fahrenheit, at which time it expands to 861 times the volume of the cryogenic liquid.

It is very tough for hundreds of scientists and engineers with an unlimited budget to make this stuff work as rocket fuel in a strictly controlled environment. I also explained about the extreme oxidation reactions of cryogenic oxygen. Among other things it either spontaneously burns, or explodes, on contact with any hydrocarbon!

Hydrogen is the smallest and lightest element in the universe. That means highly flammable hydrogen can seep through microscopic cracks. Hydrogen also has much less energy by volume than gasoline because it is so much lighter. Running an engine on hydrogen requires vastly greater quantities of it than would be necessary with gasoline.

I went through a few more technical problems with using hydrogen and pure oxygen as automobile fuel. I made it very clear this would be more expensive, less efficient, more technically complex, and extremely dangerous. I finished my presentation and asked the Congressman exactly how he proposed to overcome all these economic and engineering challenges, if he was going to replace gasoline as fuel for motor vehicles?

His answer will astound you. Remember, this man is a college-educated lawyer. Today, since he lost his job in Congress, he is teaching American government at Harvard University. Bob Inglis craned his turkey looking neck sideways, gave me a boyish smile, and dismissively explained all these things can be overcame by simply writing incentives into the next revision of the federal tax code that comes before his Ways & Means Committee!

His answer was about as stupid as saying Congress can repeal the law of gravity, but he was dead serious. Congressmen have not pretended our tax laws were fair for many decades. Nor are they primarily even for the purpose of raising revenue. The major purposes of our 7.8 million-word federal tax code is to write in incentives for certain actions - Solyndra, while penalizing others like drilling for oil. Many of them have became so bold as to assert, as did Congressman Bob Inglis, they can actually defy the laws of physics by writing incentives into the tax code.

The late Congressman Jack Kemp explained it differently. He said *"When you tax something; you get less of it. When you subsidize something else, you get more of it."* Then he nailed the problem in the American economy by concluding *"In this country, we tax work, growth, savings, and productivity; we subsidize waste, debt, non-work, consumption, and then we wonder why our economy does not work?"*

Congress and presidents have used the tax code to promote some industries, but not others. They have doled out favors to certain races, to the detriment of others. They have sought to control the crops planted by farmers, which countries we trade with, whether corn is used to feed people and animals, or to make alcohol. The list goes on and on, with thousands of decisions being made, in Washington, D.C., to micro-manage your life by using the federal tax code to as either a carrot or a stick to regulate and control you and everyone around you.

As the tea party movement transforms from protest to activist, it will be necessary for us to flex our newly acquired political muscles and demand common sense reforms of the federal tax laws. Reforms that will free our people to once more become the most productive and prosperous in the history of the world. I have spent the last forty years making my living advising small business owners on how to comply with federal tax laws and overcome economic impediments and unintended consequences built into those laws.

Here are the needed reforms:

1.) The only purpose of tax laws should be to raise revenue, and never to subsidize some activity that would not be happening in the absence of a tax subsidy.

#2.) Taxes are always a burden on someone. It is very unfair when the burden falls more on one class, one race, or one industry, than upon everyone. In the future, there should be one rate for everybody. We as a nation, can discuss through our elected representatives, what rate should be but once it is decided, there needs to be the one rate for everybody.

3.) Remembering the economics lesson from former Congressman Jack Kemp, we should not tax things we want to encourage more of. There should be no fine for the crime of working for a living. (Income tax) There should be no fine for the crime of saving and investing your money wisely in things that will appreciate in value. (Capital Gains Tax.) There should be no fine for the crime of working hard all your life to build an estate and provide a better life for your own family after you are gone. (Death Tax, a.k.a. Inheritance Tax)

#4.) The tax that is imposed needs to be short, simple, and clear enough any literate person can understand it without having to hire actuaries, attorneys, accountants, enrolled agents, and other professionals to explain how to comply with the law.

#5.) The law should be written in simple every day English, without *terms of Art* which is a legal euphemism used by lawyers when they adopt a meaning for a word that is different from what you are going to think when you read it. This is something many people may not even recognize as a problem.

Allow me to give you an example which will suffice to illustrate the greater problem. Are you an employee? Do you have employees work for you? Think about these questions, and remember your answers. Now, do you know the federal tax law has a specific definition of the word *employee* and the definition is almost certainly not what you were thinking. According to 26 USC § 3401 (c) the term *employee* is any officer, elected official, or employee of the federal government, of any state, or of a political subdivision of a state, or an officer of a corporation.

When you answered the question the first time, if you have a job and work for a paycheck, you probably assumed you were an *employee* for federal tax purposes. According to the term of art definition adopted by Congress, that assumption is only correct if you work for the government!

Conversely, if you owned your own business, and did not work for someone else, you probably thought you were not an employee. However, once again, the actual definition of an *employee* in federal tax law includes *"any officer of a corporation."* Thus, if your small business is a corporation, and you are an officer of corporation, the law says you are an *employee* for tax purposes.

Review this picture. You own a small business and are the president of your own company. You have a hired man who works for you. Under the definitions in our federal tax code, you are an *employee* and he is not!

I could take time to explain how and why all this came about, what the economic impact is, and why it has been politically expedient for Congress to resort to such convolutions of our language. Those answers are not important to understanding the necessary reforms. We need to make sure our tax laws are written in plain English where anyone with a High School education can clearly understand them.

Imagine a situation where STOP signs and YEILD RIGHT OF WAY signs had secret meanings you did not understand when you were reading them and you had to hire lawyers to explain them to you. is absurd, is it not? To know how to drive down the street, traffic signs must be clear and simple so everyone can comply with them easily.

It is just as absurd to write laws where words have special meanings you do not understand. The word *employee* is not the only such word. There are hundreds of them and whole sections of the federal tax code devoted to those definitions. In fact, it is even worse . Most of those *definitions* start off with a phrase like *"For purposes of this chapter, the word XYZ means...."* Most folks reading the definition gloss over introductory phrase as some archaic preface. The law is really saying - there are many different Chapters in the 7.8 million-word tax code and this definition of this word only applies in this Chapter! You may have to go to several other places to find different definitions for this word when it is used in another Chapter of the same law!

What if STOP signs actually meant STOP when they were on concrete roads, had a different meaning on roads paved with asphalt; and had a third meaning on unpaved roads? Then suppose the definition of a paved road did not include any road did not have at least two lanes of traffic in each direction. Suppose the definition had a completely different meaning after dark; and vehicles towing motor-boats were exempt from the provisions of STOP signs? There would be chaos on the highways. Many people would no longer drive. Those who did would get into more collisions and earn a lot more traffic citations. When prosecuting and defending those cases in court, we would employ armies of lawyers, confuse juries, and tie the court system in knots.

You are thinking Dean; all is just crazy. A STOP sign means STOP and you do not require a definition of the word STOP or any legal advice about what to do, just STOP every time. Otherwise, there would be mass confusion. Keeping it simple is the common sense way to prevent accidents and promote the efficient use of our roads.

The same principle of simplicity, clarity, and honesty, must also be applied to the words used to write federal tax laws. Otherwise, people are unsure what to do. People make plans and end up with a result they did not intend to have. Complexity and confusion impair economic activity, productivity falls, jobs are not created, and everybody in America, rich or poor, suffers as a result of the uncertainty.

English needs to be the official language in the United States and all laws need to be written in plain, clear, English that is easily understood.

#6.) We need to completely eliminate the requirement to file a tax return to pay our taxes.

#7.) We need to completely eliminate withholding of taxes from wages.

Those two reforms are accomplished by a decision to raise revenue from people spending money, not from people earning money. Remember every tax operates exactly like a fine for some activity we want to discourage. Tax spending money, rather than making money and people will make more money and save more.

The so-called Fair Tax H.R. 25; is not the answer to this needed reform. I do not want to alienate the large numbers of people who have been working hard to promote the Fair Tax, but it has several serious flaws. Two of the biggest flaws are continuing the requirement to file tax returns, and continuing socialist wealth re-distribution policies.

Both of these flaws are contained in what is known as the "prebate" provision. The way the prebate works, people with incomes below a specified amount may sign up for a new form of a welfare check to reimburse some of the cost of paying the new federal sales tax.

There are only two reasons anyone would include such a provision into the "Fair Tax" proposal. Either, they believe they must buy some votes to pass the bill. Or, they are a socialist who does not believe in free enterprise and actually wants to continue wealth redistribution schemes. Taking money from those who work, and giving it to those who do not work.

On average, we have had a major revision of our federal tax laws about every 25 years since the War Between the States in 1861. As noted above, those changes were in 1861, 1894, 1913, 1939, 1954, and, most recently in 1987. The political reality is there will be a major revision of the tax code about every 25 years. Since we will probably be stuck with any new system for another 25 years, it just makes sense to actually do it right and not settle for halfway measures.

The current economic depression has been a major contributing factor in the rise of the tea party movement. All Americans, not just tea party supporters, are seeing the detrimental results of our current tax system. Our taxes are too high, too complicated, and the socialist wealth redistribution aspects have destroyed both our economy and the work ethic of a couple of generations of our people.

The next revision of our tax laws needs to incorporate five fundamental principles:

1.) **Taxes are too high**. There are too many things being taxed and the rates are too high.

2.) **Taxes are unfair**. Currently there are between 48 and 51% of the American people who pay no income taxes at all. Over 70% of all taxes are paid by the 5% of the population in the highest income bracket. Fairness requires everyone must pay at least something to avoid destruction of the republic.

3.) **Tax laws should raise revenue**, not redistribute wealth, or regulate economic activity.

4.) **Taxes are too complicated**. The new tax system needs to be so fair and simple most Americans never again have to file any tax return.

5.) **The tax must be an indirect tax**, which complies with the constitutional requirement of uniformity throughout the United States.

There is only one type of tax will meet all these requirements, a retail sales tax on new goods. This is very similar to the Fair Tax proposal but without the prebate I believe to be a fatal flaw in the Fair Tax.

The argument has been made that Congress should create a new entitlement, or new type of welfare check, known as a prebate, to pay the poorest folks in our society so as to relieve them from paying the new sales tax imposed by the Fair Tax. The argument is a sales tax is regressive, and therefore unfair to poor people.

If regressive taxes are unfair to poor people, progressive taxes are unfair to wealthy people. Instead of continuing the trend to class warfare has divided our people and our government; why not adopt a tax requires everyone, rich or poor to share the burden equally? Instead of this us versus them mentality, let's bring this country back together where *us* once more means everybody in the United States.

We must recognize there is indeed some truth to the fact the poorest among us should be able to provide themselves with groceries and prescription medicines without paying a tax on those items. This relief can, and should, be provided. However, it must be done without bringing in fundamental unfairness, class warfare, or unnecessary complexity.

The fundamental unfairness would be to allow some Americans to avoid a tax many others still have to pay. is the very definition of unfairness. The unnecessary complexity arises when we try to determine whom we will be unfair to? Who is wealthy enough to bear an unfair burden? Who is poor enough to deserve a government handout?

The so-called Fair Tax tries, and fails, to address these questions with entitlement to the prebate welfare check. The problem is the requirement to continue to file tax returns in order to qualify for this entitlement.

Once we cross the Rubicon and require tax returns; we must then retain an army of tax collectors to examine those tax returns and enforce all the rules and regulations related to them. We are also back in the situation where most folks must hire professional help to file those returns. Our goal is to both free the people of this burden, and to have a tax system so fair nobody cheats, and so simple no returns are necessary.

The answer is simple. We do not destroy fundamental fairness by requiring the poor to pay the sales tax on necessities. We do not destroy fundamental fairness by making some folks pay a tax many others do not pay. We do not destroy the benefits of simplicity by any method that would require continuing to file tax returns, thereby keeping the bureaucracy necessary to process them.

The answer is very elegant and simple. We just exempt certain necessities of life, groceries and prescription medicines, from sales taxes.

That one sentence is the entire plan! Nobody, rich or poor, should have to pay a sales tax on groceries or prescription medicines. Period. That is the whole, entire plan.

There is nothing at all complicated about this plan. There is nothing unfair. Nothing in this plan is unconstitutional. There is nothing in this plan not already being done every day.

Look no further than the State of Texas. Groceries and prescription medicines are exempt from state's sales tax. When you buy groceries in a store, the purchase is rung up on a non-taxable cash register key. When you buy a taxable item, perhaps alcohol or tobacco, the purchase is rung up on the taxable key on the cash register.

Pause a minute and marvel at this simple but elegant solution to all necessary tax reforms. When you walk into a store and make a retail purchase, it is the item being sold that is classified as either taxable or non taxable. All purchasers are treated exactly the same. Nothing can be more fair or simple. You are not asked if you are affluent or impecunious. You are not asked if you speak the English language. You are not asked your age [unless you are purchasing alcohol.] You are not asked if you are an illegal alien. You do not have to file any sort of sales tax return.

The Texas Legislature, in its collective wisdom, has always chosen to exempt groceries and prescription medicines from requirement for paying a sales tax. Notice the word groceries. Not everything sold in a grocery store is tax exempt. The requirement medicines must be prescription means the legislature has chosen to tax over the counter medicines. It is certainly possible the exact same bottle of aspirin or cough syrup will be taxable if the customer buys it without any prescription, and non-taxable if it is purchased with a prescription.

Do physicians in Texas write prescriptions for common over-the-counter medicines more frequently than doctors in other states that tax all medicines? I am sure they do, and it does not hurt a thing. The legislature, bowing to the will of the people, has wisely decided to trust the discretion of physicians.

The tea party movement is nothing more, or less, than the majority of the American people deciding they are fed up with the corruption and financial excesses of our political system; and engaging in some long overdue hands-on management of our elected officials.

It is high time the American people reminded our Congress the *"heavy, progressive, or graduated, tax on incomes"* comes from the <u>Communist Manifesto</u>, not the United States constitution. We need to demand a complete overhaul of our tax system. Replace all current forms of federal taxes with a national tax on the retail sales of new goods. This is constitutional, simple to administer and places the economic incentive to work, save, invest and hire people, in the correct place.

As Ronald Reagan once observed *"A rising tide lifts all boats."* With the repeal of federal taxes on corporation income, individual income, capital gains, and repeal of the death tax, we will see real, solid economic growth unprecedented in the history of the world.

Chapter XII

Currency Reform!

Our founding fathers understood there were two ways to destroy the economy of our republic. One way to destroy the new government would be to burden it with debt in time of peace. The other way to destroy this nation is to debase its currency.

The men who met at Independence Hall in Philadelphia to draft our constitution were well educated. They were familiar with the history of the world and the effects both coinage, and paper substitutes for coinage, had on the commerce, peace, and prosperity of nations.

The use of *money*, more particularly gold and silver coinage, has been the foundation of modern civilization. It expanded commercial transactions, and empowered technological innovation. The specific monetary reform I believe my friends in the tea party movement must demand is a return to honest, constitutional money - circulating gold and silver coinage.

To evaluate this proposal, you will need the wisdom of our founding fathers. Wisdom comes from two sources, knowledge and experience. To gain more wisdom before formulating a political proposal to reform our currency, let's increase our knowledge of what money is, and the purpose it serves. Let's also look briefly at the role money has played in the history of nations.

Our ancient ancestors were wandering nomads living off the land as hunters and gatherers, for many thousands of years. In such primitive conditions there was not much trade or commerce. When there was, it was accomplished by means of barter. A hunter bartering his excess game with another man who owned an excess of arrowheads may have been a good trade for each man.

We have heard commerce referred to as trade. Years ago, it was common for people to say a man *traded* at some particular store, meaning he was a customer of store. Inventory was often referred to as *trade goods*. These were linguistic throwbacks to the days when people with no money existed by means of pure barter, each literally *trading* his excess goods, for those of another.

Trade, or barter, was the crude foundation of what would come to be known as civilization. Living in small tribes and family groups who each traded what they acquired or produced in excess, was certainly easier than living off the land.

Pure trade or barter still had numerous limitations and drawbacks. When the goods you had for trading were foodstuffs, they were often perishable. There were also times when what you had to trade, and what you needed to acquire, were simply not easily found.

Our ancestors eventually learned there was great usefulness in anything they could carry around that was durable, scarce, and valuable to others. The fisherman, whose only *trade goods* were fish, was limited because his *trade goods* were perishable. He was faced with the need to spend it or lose it. More durable goods, salt, whiskey, tobacco, tools, weapons, were each more useful than a mess of fish, because they lasted longer.

These more durable *trade goods* possessed two of the three attributes of what would come to be known as money. They were durable, and valuable. They did not yet possess the third attribute of money because they were not a standard unit for the measurement of value - the final attribute of money. Think of these early *trade goods* as *pre-money*. Look at the life of a hunter, first without any *pre-money*, and then with some *pre-money* and you will understand the usefulness of pre-money.

The hunter wishes to purchase bread from the baker. His only tender of payment is a freshly killed bear. Both the hunter and the baker agree the bear is worth many times the cost of a loaf of bread. The baker has nothing to offer in exchange except more bread. The hunter does not need 100 loaves of bread. The baker has no other way to 'make change.'

Even worse, the baker may have recently sold bread to another hunter for a bear, and now has no use for a second bear. Under pure barter there are numerous inefficiencies of this nature, limiting its effectiveness.

Killing a bear, exchanging it for 100 loaves of bread, bartering 75 loaves of bread for two overcoats, and finally bartering one coat for a new spear, with which to hunt, is very time consuming and inefficient. Life would be simpler, more efficient and everyone more productive if it was possible under all circumstances to strike one bargain, fair to both parties, and obtain needed goods and services.

This is only possible if the buyer and seller each have something durable, scarce, and valuable, the other person wants and needs. It would be particularly useful to have some product with which to barter which would be universally accepted by anyone else.

In addition to being useful, this perfect barter commodity should also be easily divisible into portions of different sizes to facilitate transactions. The perfect medium for promotion of commerce should be durable as well. Carrying around a freshly killed bear is not a good way to possess wealth. The perfect barter item must have a high value for a small weight of the commodity. Something should be worth as much as a freshly killed bear but weigh only a few ounces, so as to be portable.

When there are durable goods circulating among trading partners which are not always consumed, but often used to facilitate trade, everyone benefits and civilization flourishes.

Now the bear hunter in our earlier example only needs to engage in two transactions. First he sells his bear carcass for some *pre-money*. Then, because *pre-money* is durable, scarce, valuable, portable, and divisible; he can simply carry around some *pre-money* at all times to engage in any needful transaction. The use of *pre-money* to facilitate transactions is a clear advance over straight barter. There have been any number of substances used to serve the purpose of *pre-money*.

Early American Indians placed a high value on *wampum* made from sea shells. Therefore wampum was very useful as *pre-money* in barter based societies. Early European settlers who often engaged in commerce with Indian tribes sometimes adopted wampum as well. The purpose of this chapter is to chronicle the development of *money* and it's synergistic impact on the development of modern civilization.

I would be remiss if I did not point out there were cultural and spiritual aspects to the development of civilization as well. A detailed study of those cultural and spiritual influences is mostly outside the scope of this work.

In the case of *wampum* in particular, there were considerable cultural differences between the Indians and the Europeans. Europeans saw *wampum* as *Indian money* and focused upon its use in commerce. *Wampum* was useful to the Indians as a decorative wearing apparel that symbolized social status. Gifts, including *wampum*, were often exchanged as signs of friendship.

Wampum consisted of beads made from seashells. There were two types. The more common, and thus less valuable, were the white beads. The black or purple beads, being rarer were several times as valuable. Because there were two colors of *wampum* could be woven into wearing apparel, it was possible to create pictographs and geometric designs in the finished products. Many of these *wampum* artworks symbolized spiritual principles. Others were used to solemnize and memorialize treaties between the several Indian nations, or between an Indian nation and British, Dutch, or later Americans.

The primary usefulness of *wampum* was ornamentation. Other substances have been monetized because they too served a useful purpose. Salt, tools, tobacco, beaver pelts, gunpowder and whiskey are just a few examples of substances which have been used in trade to various degrees. The overwhelming favorites through all of history have been *gold* or *silver*. Sometimes a naturally occurring alloy of *gold* and *silver* known as *electrum* was used.

Gold is a naturally occurring yellow metal with very unusual properties. There are a number of reasons for the value placed on *gold* by every society through history. *Gold* is comparatively rare. Rarity alone does not account for all of the allure of *gold*. It is also very useful in ways as diverse as jewelry, dentistry, electronics, medicine, art, corrosion resistance, and of course *money*. *Gold* is chemically inert and highly resistant to oxidation. It may be hammered into very thin sheets, drawn into fine wire, stamped into *coins* and worked in many other ways.

Gold fits the need for a medium of exchange perfectly. It has been valued by every society in history and is durable. Small amounts are quite valuable, making it easily portable. *Gold* may be divided into portions of any required size, making it useful in transactions of any size. Once the mighty hunter sold his bear carcass for gold, he can now infinitely preserve the wealth the bear carcass represented.

Other metals have also been used to facilitate commercial exchanges between people. The most important of these are *silver, electrum, platinum, copper,* and *aluminum.*

We read in the book of Genesis Abraham bought a field with a cave upon it to use as a burial place for his wife Sarah [Genesis 23:16]. The Bible tells us the bargain was struck for 400 shekels of *silver,* and Abraham weighed out the correct amount of *silver.*

What allowed men to take the final step from the use of *pre-money* to facilitate trade and barter, into our modern civilization? The answer is the invention of *money,* specifically go*ld and silver coinage.* What advantage does actual *coinage* have over the *pre-money* we have already looked at?

Can you imagine your wife paying for a dress and having to *weigh out* the right amount of *gold* or s*ilver* to pay for the dress? Primitive and inefficient right? You bet! Who wants to carry around scales to weigh their medium of barter? Who is willing to trust the scales of the merchant? Who can prove, the purity of the *gold* or *silver* offered in exchange for the dress? How much time and inconvenience are involved in the assay (the proverbial acid test) and the weighing for each transaction? Who bears the burden of this cost? The buyer? The seller? Is this cost explicitly acknowledged and its burden is then bargained between the parties? Is it merely an implicit cost of doing business? In the latter case, one or both parties simply figured it into the price they negotiated.

Over three thousand years ago someone thought of a better way to do things. Suppose some very well trusted person took a piece of *gold,* assayed it and placed a mark upon it to show the result of assay. Then weighed the piece of *gold,* now of a known purity, and placed another mark on it to show the weight. Now, if fifty thousand people each had such a piece of *gold* of the exact weight and purity required for a baseball ticket; paying at the gate speeds up considerably. In fact, the transaction gets very easy.

A couple of things were usually necessary to insure the assay and weight were done fairly and accurately. First, the trusted party under whose authority it was done was usually the king or other ruler. Second, king or ruler granted himself a monopoly on the business of assaying and weighing lumps of *gold*. He also prohibited counterfeiting his marks for weight and purity. Finally there was a considerable penalty for disobeying this law. The most common penalty being death.

With lumps of *gold* of a known weight and purity, we are now very close to having modern *money*. Almost but no cigar. Mark Twain once remarked the difference between the right word and almost the right word was the difference between lightening and the lightening bug!

Let's go ahead and call the King's establishment for weighing and assaying lumps of *gold* the Royal Mint. What are the odds of fifty thousand people each bringing in a lump of *gold* to be weighed and assayed were all found to have the exact same purity and the exact same weight? Somewhere between slim and none. Unless, of course, the King knew the usefulness of such identical lumps of *gold* to commerce.

It is a simple matter to just order *gold* of a known purity is melted and struck into identical pieces. There are numerous benefits to the kingdom in this process being adopted. The King finds this to be a good place to put his graven image. The mint charges a fee, called seniorage, for producing *coins* from precious metals.

These objects each containing an identical weight and purity of a valuable substance - usually *silver* or *gold* - are known as *coins* or *money*. The most vital function of *money* is to act as a standard or measure of value. In order to accomplish purpose a unit of value must be established. Once such a standard is established, *coins* will be struck with the value of unit of measure. It is also common to strike *coins* are multiples or fractions of unit as well.

We see *money* has two components, *coinage* and a law specifying a unit for the measure of value. It is easy to demonstrate *coins*, even coins containing *gold* or *silver*, would not be money in the absence of the law that defines a unit of measure. There are numerous companies who strike *gold* medallions privately. Most are simply convenient ways to sell bullion and a few are struck as commemorative or strictly numismatic items. Other privately minted *coins* have even been used in commercial promotions as a form of advertising.

Coins have been around at least since 700 B.C. and probably longer. Early coins were struck in Lydia and Ionia (modern western Turkey) from *electrum*, a naturally occurring alloy of *gold* and *silver*. In China *coins* were struck from at least 600 B.C.

Initially these *coins* were bronze representations of tools like spades and knives. Probably because tools had been useful in barter before *coins* came into general circulation. Early Chinese *coins* were struck which were round in shape with a square hole in the middle of them. They were called cash and that is the origin of our word cash.

These cash were probably representative of the wheel, another common early tool. The round *coins* with the square hole in the center proved to be a durable design and were in use for the next 2,400 years, until about 1911.

The use of *coinage* was spread from ancient Greece by the Armies of Alexander the Great (356 –323 BC) to all the lands he conquered.

Coins are among the richest sources for the art and history of ancient civilizations. *Coins* sometimes have images of animals, useful tools, gods, and most often rulers. Early *coins* were not dated in the modern sense but the years of their manufacture may be deduced from inscriptions and images of rulers whose reign occurred between known dates. *Coins* have actually been used in India to determine when a particular ruler was in Power. The ancient Vedic scriptures gave several conflicting stories of who ruled India at a particular time. Archeologists have been able to determine which account was correct by examining *coins* minted by ruler.

Coinage was also used to decipher an ancient language. In the year 1835 James Prinsep was able to decipher the ancient Brahmi language of India by studying bi-lingual Indo-Greek inscriptions on *coins*, sort of a numismatic Rosetta stone.

In addition to their own images, Roman Emperors often struck coins with the inscription FIDES MILITVM attesting to the loyalty of the army to Emperor. One of the principal uses of such *coins* was to pay the army. Ironically some minor usurpers to the Imperial purple would be completely unknown to history if it were not for such *coins* they minted—shortly before being executed by the 'loyal' army. The tribute penny mentioned in the Bible was a silver *denarius* of the Emperor Tiberius (14-37 AD). The thirty pieces of *silver* paid to Judas to betray the Lord were *silver tetradrachm* minted in Tyre.

Many issues of *coins* proved to be very durable and stable. The *solidus* of Byzantium was first issued by the Emperor Constantine the Great (Born 274 AD, reign 306-337 AD) and continued to be minted and circulate at almost the identical weight and fineness for the next 1,000 years. The Italians are credited with the invention and use of the first mills, circa 1500, for punching out uniform round metal disks or planchets and using screw presses for impressing designs upon them. The first mint in the New World was established after the Spanish conquest of Mexico City in 1535. That was 235 years before the U.S. Mint was established in 1792!

Unlike the Spanish, the English did not provide for the minting of coins in the new world. Thus the English and French in America were left to use barter, *wampum,* tobacco, whiskey, Spanish milled *dollars*, foreign *coins* or what ever they could find as a means of exchange.

The foundation of modern civilization rests upon the invention of *money*. So, you are asking, is *coinage* really on par with the discovery of fire? Is it equal in importance with harnessing controlled nuclear fission reactions? Is *coinage* as important to civilization as the wheel or the airplane? The answer is, you bet!

Without *coins,* our modern trade based civilization becomes impossible. Without trade the necessities of life, food and shelter, are so difficult to obtain there is no waking moment not devoted their acquisition. Without leisure time there is no development of technology, no mastery of the environment. No spiritual development. No culture, literature, or arts.

Is it possible to store the wealth you accumulate and trade with others in the absence of *coinage*? Only in a primitive, slow, difficult and inefficient manner. Imagine being paid in goods, perhaps some of what ever you are helping to produce. Then having to take those goods and try, to pay your bills each week. Try to use those goods for all your daily purchases.

Would convenience stores become an oxymoron? Would taking the children to McDonalds be any easier? How about stopping for gas? Paying the neighbor boy to mow your lawn? Do you see a pattern here?

Clearly commerce, therefore modern civilization, depends upon the orderly transaction of exchanges of goods and services made possible only by *coins*. When something is this powerful, this useful, and this necessary; we don't leave it in the hands of an individual. We must come together and agree upon how it will be created and used.

Coming together, collectively, to work in groups for the common good is the most basic definition of government. For thousands of years men recognized there are certain things difficult, or even impossible, for individuals acting alone to accomplish efficiently. These things including, building roads, fighting fires, punishing thieves, and providing for the national defense, are each best done through collective efforts.

Those collective efforts are government. When we discuss the need for such social organization in theoretical terms it all sounds very logical and efficient. We can pity the savage with no government the way we pity him for not knowing how to use fire to cook his meat. In the real world it has often been observed government, like fire, is a dangerous servant, and a fearful master.

There are as many ways to form a government, as there are to structure a barter transaction. That is to say, if you can think of it, someone has probably done it somewhere. [...there is no new thing under the sun. *Ecclesiastes* 1: 9]

What is clear, for better or worse, is very important things are usually controlled by the government. This may be positively stated as individuals recognizing such important powers should not be concentrated in too few hands. It may also be negatively stated as government seeking to control individuals by keeping power concentrated in the hands of the government. For whatever reason, *coinage*, with a few exceptions we will discuss later, has usually been a government monopoly.

We might assume if *coinage* allows all modern economic activity, and it does, our ancestors shortly after 600 B.C. should quickly have developed steam engines. In a few more generations they could have mastered flight and well before the birth of Christ, nuclear power and space flight might have been quite commonplace and ordinary. What happened along the yellow brick road to utopia?

I just finished reading a book on financial planning. The author describes a businessman who owns a grocery store. He allows his wife to take groceries out the back door instead of paying for them. Seeing this example, his employees also begin to take groceries out the back door instead of paying for them. Soon the grocer is in bankruptcy.

Meanwhile another grocer makes his wife pay for her groceries. His employees don't steal from him. Soon he opens more locations. Eventually he has many stores, provides employment for thousands of people and groceries to hundreds of thousands. The same author tells the story of a bank in Midland Texas in the 1980's made insider loans to its directors, who speculated in the booming oil business. The oil boom went bust. These men defaulted on their "loans" and as a result the bank went bankrupt. Meanwhile, in the same tough economic times for the oil industry, banks were operated honestly still made profits. They opened branches, bought other banks and grew in size, strength and power.

Why, with the miracle of *coinage*, did we not proceed directly to modern civilization in a few hundred years? Because *coinage* has been a government monopoly and governments steal. Governments do not tell the truth. Governments rob their people. Let's look at the long, sad, history of governments in control of the *money* supply.

At the time of the Roman conquest of Egypt (21 A.D.) the principal *coin* in circulation was the Roman *tetradrachm*. At first, this coin was 50% *silver,* about an inch in diameter, and weighed 180 grains. There were also *bronze* coins in circulation with lower values. Beginning in 21 AD these *tetradrachm* were steadily debased. There was less and less *silver* content in coins supposedly had the same value year after year.

By 296 AD the silver content of the tetradrachm was less than one percent, the coin was now only about 3/4 of an inch in diameter and weighed only 90 grains. The depreciation of the silver content and purchasing power of the tetradrachm had declined so much by 180 AD lower denomination bronze coins were no longer struck and did not circulate after date. Politicians had figured out coins could be made to look like earlier coins but contain less silver. If stealing the silver was done slowly, in this case over a 271 year period, and *laws* were passed to say the new coins were just as valuable as the old.... Well, those politicians were doing the same thing as the store owner's wife who carried groceries out the back door without paying for them. That is to say, they were stealing by debasing the silver content of the coins.

When crooked individuals steal from the government by making cheap [bad] coins which superficially resemble genuine coins; the government says it is *counterfeiting*. When the government does the exact same thing, they call it *currency reform*. Was this problem confined only to the Romans and the Egyptians?

The ancient Chinese produced coins that were maintained for 2,400 years at the same fineness and weight. As a result these coins circulated in commerce. They were not restricted to China and were used in Japan and other countries as well.

In 708 A.D. the Japanese imported and used Chinese coinage. Soon the warlords, known as *Shoguns,* realized the manufacture of coinage was both a way to consolidate power, and a way to make a profit.

They began to mint coins, which, at first, mimicked the weight and design of the popular Chinese coins. Over time the *Shogun* debased the coinage, making coins with less weight carry the same nominal value as earlier good coinage. The result was price inflation followed by further debasement of the coinage, followed by more price inflation, in a vicious circle, until the coins were worthless. The Japanese people, unable to obtain the better quality Chinese coins reverted back, for a time, to the more primitive barter system, abandoning the use of coinage altogether.

It is beyond the scope of this chapter to write a detailed history of world money and the myriad of numismatic items that have been created over the past twenty four centuries. It is informative to look at the consistent record of monarchs debasing coinage over time, often as a way to pay for wars.

Rulers have understood for centuries, when they debase the coinage too much, the debasement drives prices up causing "inflation". When the supply of debased coinage is increased to still higher levels, it eventually ceases to circulate completely. Debasing coinage raises revenue for the government while defrauding the people who are forced by *legal tender* laws to accept coins with an intrinsic value far below face value. At other times, monarchs leave the coinage relatively unadulterated, and simply raise taxes or impose new types of taxes.

The English system of coinage is very alien to modern Americans. It was gibberish to me as well, until I made a study of it. I have read passages in classical literature about coins called by exotic names like farthings, crowns, sovereigns, guineas and so forth. Let's get a general understanding of what these coins were and the relative values of each to the other. These are terms were very familiar to our founding fathers. George Washington and Benjamin Franklin grew up in a world where they were money.

The farthing is a word literally means a fourth of a thing and derived from early customs of breaking the English silver penny into four parts to make small change. Thus early farthings and half pence were literally silver pennies had been broken into halves or quarters. Early farthing and halfpence coins were also silver

Americans today think of a penny as a copper coin with Lincoln's face on it. Remember these English "pennies" or pence were silver coins about the same size and weight as our U.S. dime. And they were worth what our dime was worth when it was still silver before 1965.

On Thursday, August 1, 1672 Charles II issued the first copper farthings and halfpence. It is interesting to note the intrinsic value of the copper in these coins was only about 1/2 the face value of the coins. Officially, this discouraged melting coinage for bullion. Of course, unofficially, if you are the King and you can give people half the value of something, you keep the other half of the value.

Even Kings faced the occasional tax revolt. It is a lot more politically expedient to simply give the people debased coinage than to issue money at its full face value and then try to tax it at 50%. Coinage was frequently debased by the government as a method of raising revenue without having to impose taxes. Other common reasons for debasing coinage were to pay for warfare or to pay reparations to foreign governments.

One of the earliest examples was the English monarch Aethelred II who reigned for forty-eight years from 968 AD to 1016 AD. He agreed to pay a bribe to the Danes not to raid the English coasts and rob his people. This payment was known as the Dane Geld and Aethelred II, paid £ 155,000 in coins that were debased and contained only a small fraction of precious metal. Interestingly, these coins were accepted in payment, and used by the Danes, because the Danes had debased their own coinage even more.

The first English "Penny" was minted in 866 A.D. in 92.5% silver (Sterling). Each Penny was 1/240th of an English pound of 5,400 grains. There was 22.5 grains of silver in each coin. In the early years the practice of farthing, or breaking, these coins into four pieces to make change was, very common, even though prohibited by law.

When William of Normandy decided in 1066 to invade England he financed his conquest of King Harold with money raised debasing the content of Norman coinage. William the Conqueror also instituted the Doomsday Book in which everything in England was counted for the purpose of being taxed. Interestingly, William did not debase English coinage after the conquest.

The proclamation of 1108 A.D. required all Pennies to be accepted in trade, a forerunner of our modern legal tender laws. Since Pennies were silver coins in those days, they were often notched to detect counterfeits with copper cores. A royal proclamation issued December 25th 1124 required all *moneyers* to stand trial in Winchester for the crime of debasing coinage. This was known as the *Assize of Moneyers*. The penalty was to have your right hand cut off. About half of those tried were found guilty and were mutilated in the hand or the genitals.

Henry III (reign 1216—1272) debased the currency to support his lavish spending and finance his long running feuds with the Papacy. He also "borrowed" from the Jews, then threatened them with prison unless the debts were forgiven.

In 1279 the first half pennies were struck and they would be minted for the next four hundred years. By 1412 A.D. the amount of silver in each penny had been reduced from 22.5 grains to only 15 grains. In 1472 A.D. this was reduced to 12 grains or slightly more than half the original silver content.

While the term penny is familiar to us, we can deduce other amounts by the sound of the word. Thus, tupence was two pennies, threepence was three pennies and sixpence was six pennies. Other names were less intuitive for Americans, the groat was four pennies and the schilling twelve pennies. A crown is five schillings, a pound twenty schillings, and a guinea twenty-one schillings. The farthing and the halfpence were brass coins. Pennies through schillings were silver coins; with the double crown, pound, and guinea being gold coins. There were also two guinea and five guinea coins, also in gold.

Between 1500 and 1560 as coinage was debased further, prices of food doubled, then doubled again. Thomas Woolsey debased the currency in 1526 to help Henry VIII finance his war with France. In 1544 the silver content of the Penny was reduced to 1/5 of what it had been under Henry VII.

Elizabeth I reformed the coinage with a completely new issue in 1560—61. Debasement of coinage was not exclusively an English problem. On December 31, 1596 Phillip II of Spain removed the 30% silver backing of Spanish billon coins. After complaints from the nobility he restored a symbolic 0.3% (three tenths of one percent) silver content to the coinage on February 1, 1597.

His son, Phillip III removed even 0.3% in 1602.

During the Seven Years War 1756—1763 the Prussians were able to obtain genuine dies from which Polish coins were struck. These dies were used to strike counterfeits of very low intrinsic value. These circulated as an economic weapon of war.

Our founding fathers clearly understood the long history of money, both periods of prosperity under sound currency, as well as war, poverty, and misery flowing from periods where governments debased the currency. Our founders also knew the history of paper substitutes for honest money.

The history of paper substitutes for money starts long ago, and far away, in China. The Chinese developed many inventions and innovations over the long course of human history. They are credited with inventions as diverse as the umbrella and gunpowder.

As early as the Han Dynasty (circa 118 B.C.) the Chinese were using Pai-Lu P'i-pi or *white deer skin money* about one foot square to write upon for a representation of money. These large deerskin parchment documents were not true banknotes and did not circulate in commerce because of the large denomination 40,000 cash. The *cash* was a small bronze coin of low value with a square hole in the middle.

The Tang Dynasty (618—907 A.D.) instituted *flying cash* around 800 A.D. Called *flying cash* because the paper notes could blow away in the wind, something that was not a problem with bronze coins. The *flying cash* of the Tang Dynasty was still issued only in very large denominations. The Tang government used *flying cash* certificates for large government purchases from merchants in distant provinces and the certificates could be converted to actual cash. Again, these were not circulating as a medium of exchange. They were similar to our $100,000 Federal Reserve Notes which were never issued into circulation and only exchanged between Federal Reserve Banks to settle large accounts.

True banknotes issued for circulation did not come into existence until the Song Dynasty (960—1279 A.D.) when they were authorized to be printed by wealthy merchants and financiers in the Szechuan Province.

These notes had pictures of houses, trees and people, they were printed in two colors of ink, red and black. They contained the seals of the issuing bank affixed to each bill. After 1023 A.D. these private banknotes were withdrawn and thereafter only official government notes were allowed to circulate. Song Dynasty notes did not depreciate in value because they were backed 100% by cash reserves and the notes and coins circulated freely and were interchangeable. The Emperor also punished counterfeiting by death. In 1183 A.D. a printer who made 2,600 fake notes in six months was sentenced to death.

After the Ch'in Dynasty (1115—1234 A.D.) occupied northern China they followed the Song Dynasty practice and established a

Bureau of Paper Currency in Kaifeng as the central government agency in charge of all issues. One modern researcher Qui Shiyu of the Harbin Academy of Sciences maintains that prominent Jewish businessmen assisted the Ch'in Dynasty in the creation of paper currency. He notes the currency was printed on crude jute paper and none of it has survived. However the copper plates used to print it have survived and one is in the Chinese Museum of History. The plates show several "fanye" design elements which "*only belonged to the Jewish Nation*".

Historical evidence shows a group of Jewish traders came to China in the middle of the 10th century. Most of them reached what is today Kaifeng, in Henan Province, which was the capital of the southern Song Dynasty (1127– 1279 A.D.) . This was the most prosperous business and trading metropolis of the time. During the Ch'in Dynasty little thought was given to backing the currency and inflation soared. As paper currency became worthless the economy floundered, people secretly reverted to the use of bronze, silver and even barter as a medium of exchange. Soon afterward the Mongols invaded and conquered China, establishing the Yuan Dynasty (1264 —1368 A.D.) Historians believe the hyperinflated currency and weakened economy made the conquest of China by Genghis Kahn possible.

The first paper notes of the Yuan Dynasty were printed in 1260 A.D. by Kublai Khan the grandson of Genghis Khan. Known as "Mulberry Money" because paper the notes were printed on were made from grinding the pulp of a white layer between the outer bark and inner wood of the mulberry tree.

European traveler Marco Polo arrived around 1279 A.D. and was truly amazed at the process used to make Mulberry 'money'. The notes were elaborately printed with the promises of the government to pay as well as dire warnings counterfeiting of the notes was a death penalty offense. Then various officials carefully affixed seals to the notes with great solemnity.

The notes were quickly inflated being completely nonconvertible into coinage. They only circulated because refusing to accept them was a death penalty offense. Marco Polo also noted all foreign traders arriving in China were required by the Great Khan to deposit all silver, gold, and pearls, with the Imperial government in exchange for "*liberal*" payment in Mulberry money.

Our Founding Fathers were educated men. They understood history. They knew things even stranger than the bark of Mulberry trees have been used as substitutes for actual money. In England, for about 726 years, broken sticks with little notches carved on them had been used as a substitute for money.

Our Founders also remembered this was a disaster that resulted in great economic misery and fraud. Later in 1834 it would even lead to the burning down of the British House of Parliament.

These sticks were known as *Talley* sticks. First used during the reign of King Henry I around 1100 A.D. A *Talley* stick was nothing more than a strip of wood usually about 18 inches in length. Remember, in the 1100's most people, other than the clergy, even Kings and Queens, were completely illiterate. If everyone in government and business was illiterate, it would not be particularly useful to write contracts, promissory notes or receipts for deposits. The answer in England was to use a Talley stick to show money had been given by the lender and received by the borrower. Notches cut into the stick to indicated the amount of money represented. Then, the Talley stick was split lengthwise. The lender kept half and the borrower kept the other half.

At a later date the two halves of the Talley stick could be re-joined and would fit together perfectly. The grain and other natural imperfections in the wood were a low-tech way to prevent any fraud. The longer portion of the stick, known as the *stock*, was retained by the lender. This was the origin of the word *stock* we use today to describe shares of ownership in a company. The shorter portion was known as the *foil* and it was retained by the borrower. This is the origin of phrase *getting the short end of the stick*, meaning to go into debt. Talley sticks were used by goldsmiths as receipts for gold deposited with them.

In Medieval England, it was customary for the King to collect taxes twice a year, once at Easter and again in the fall after crops were harvested. Since there was little actual money in circulation and much of the economic activity was still based upon barter, taxes were most often paid with farm produce rather than in actual money.

The King's tax collectors would assess an amount, carved on a Talley stick. Later in the year when the tax was paid, the halves of the Talley stick were matched and then both halves were retired from circulation. In the year 1660 Charles II was restored to the throne of England.

Charles II had lavish spending habits, and fought several expensive wars. He repeatedly imposed unpopular taxes to raise revenues. Always short of money, Charles hit upon the scheme of using the Talley sticks, representing future tax revenues to the crown, as collateral for loans of money from Goldsmiths. Naturally Charles had to *discount* the Talley sticks; that is, accept less than the full face value of each stick. The Goldsmiths made a handsome profit by redeeming the sticks later in the year when Charles collected taxes.

As time went on, Charles had more lavish spending habits and occasionally another war to pay for. It became necessary to *discount* the Talley sticks more steeply in order to borrow real money against them. The goldsmiths ran their own crooked scam at the same time. They used these Talley sticks, with the implied promise of future tax revenues, as backing for paper script they issued to make purchases.

In effect, these English goldsmiths were the forerunners of modern banks and were issuing worthless bank notes backed by very little gold, and, mostly the promises of future collections memorialized on the Talley sticks they were buying from the King at deep *discounts*.

The King pretended not to notice the frauds of these early proto-bankers because they continued to purchase his worthless sticks for gold. Eventually Tally sticks were discounted so heavily they brought Charles very little revenue. He then began to simply counterfeit massive numbers of the now almost worthless Talley sticks.

Like every other fiat currency in history, Talley sticks resulted in price inflation as their actual value fell to nothing, they finally stopped circulating, and those who had accepted them as currency or collateral were wiped out financially. The system of using Talley sticks was not completely abolished until 1826. Then in 1834 it was decided the many thousands of Talley sticks still in possession of the government should be destroyed.

They were ordered destroyed in a wood burning stove in the House of Parliament. The stovepipe overheated, set the paneling of the walls on fire, and the fire spread, burning the Parliament building to the ground.

The example of paper substitutes for money most on the minds of our Founding Fathers would have been their own experience with a Continental Currency. During our Revolutionary War, both the Continental Congress and each of the thirteen Colonies issued its own paper notes promising to pay money at a later date.

This is known as a *fiat* currency, meaning it has no actual value, is not convertible into anything of value, and usually is issued without anything of real value being required to be held in reserve as backing for it. The word *fiat* is a Latin word, meaning *let it be done*. A *fiat* currency has value only because the government is willing to accept it in payment of taxes, or the government has adopted a Legal Tender Act, or law requiring the *fiat* currency to be accepted.

In every case three things happen:

First, the government promises that the fiat currency will relieve a shortage of honest money, and universal prosperity will result.

Second, it is usually done to pay for some temporary emergency, most often to fund a war. Promises are made as soon as the war is over, or the crisis is ended, all the worthless notes will be redeemed at face value for honest money at some future date.

Third, politicians, once given the power to issue fiat substitutes for money, realize they basically have the power to create money substitutes out of nothing. This leads to all sorts of utopian ideas for things can be built, or bought, with this *free money*. As more and more worthless *fiat* money is poured into the economy, people prefer honest money in the form of gold or silver coins. Soon every transaction has two prices, there is the price in honest gold or silver money, and the much higher price in *fiat* currency.

I will sell my horses to the Army for $20 each, in gold. I do not really want to accept the *fiat* currency in lieu of gold, so my price in so called *paper money* is $100 per horse. As more and more paper is printed and issued into circulation, I want $1,000 in paper for something worth $20 in gold. Eventually I will need $10,000 in paper for $20 in gold. Finally the *paper money* is worthless, and nobody will sell anything for so called *paper money*. The *fiat* currency is worthless and no longer circulates.

During our Revolution, soldiers in Washington's Continental Army were required to accept the fiat Continental Currency as payment for service. To protest this fraud, some actually sewed the Continental Currency into clothing they wore. Continental notes were used as wallpaper, and even burned for firewood because they were useless as money. General George Washington complained at one time it took a wagon load of continental currency to purchase a wagon load of supplies for his Army.

This fiat currency actually changed the English language here in America. Something completely useless or worthless was said to be *not worth a Continental damn*, alluding to the worthless currency. Each of the Thirteen Colonies issued its own fiat currency, resulting in hyper-inflation of prices as denominated in the fiat currency. This was much worse in New England than in the middle Colonies, but there was no colony whose fiat currency remained on par with gold coin.

Our founders met from May to September 1787 at Independence Hall in Philadelphia to draft our federal constitution. Sent to Philadelphia to amend and improve the Articles of Confederation, the delegates, meeting in secret, decided to scrap the Articles of Confederation and write a whole new plan of government.

The portion of the document that became Article I, Section 8, Clause 5, dealing with money was debated, and adopted, on August 16th. The deliberations in the Constitutional Convention were done in secret behind locked doors. Armed guards were posted to keep away eavesdroppers. There was no official journal of the convention made.

One member of the convention kept a journal, in which he made notes about the proceedings. One day the delegates broke for lunch and this unfortunate fellow left his journal in a public restaurant. Another delegate saw the journal, retrieved it, and since it bore no name, gave it to General George Washington.

Washington gave all the delegates a stern lecture about their solemn promises to keep the proceedings secret. He then laid the offending journal on the dais and invited its owner to come forward and reclaim it. The journal lay there for the next several weeks and no one would claim it. Such was the secrecy that surrounded the creation of our constitution.

There was only one journal of the day-to-day discussions and votes of the delegates which has survived and was later published, that of future President James Madison. Here are the actual words from Madison's diary for August 16, 1787:

Mr. GOVr. MORRIS moved to strike out "and emit bills on the credit of the United States" — If the United States had credit such bills would be unnecessary: if they had not, unjust and useless.

Mr. BUTLER, 2ds. the motion.

Mr. MADISON, will it not be sufficient to prohibit the making them a tender? This will remove the temptation to emit them with unjust views. And promissory notes in shape may in some emergencies be best.

Mr. Govr. MORRIS. striking out the words will leave room still for notes of a responsible minister which will do all the good without the mischief. The Monied interest will oppose the plan of Government, if paper emissions be not prohibited.

Mr. GHORUM was for striking out, without inserting any prohibition. if the words stand they may suggest and lead to the measure.

Col. MASON had doubts on the subject. Congress he thought would not have the power unless it were expressed. Though he had a mortal hatred to paper money, yet as he could not foresee all emergencies, he was unwilling to tie the hands of the Legislature. He observed the late war could not have been carried on, had such a prohibition existed.

Mr. GHORUM. The power as far as it will be necessary or safe, is involved in of borrowing.

Mr. MERCER was a friend to paper money, though in the present state and temper of America, he should neither propose nor approve of such a measure. He was consequently opposed to a prohibition of it altogether. It will stamp suspicion on the Government to deny it a discretion on this point. It was impolitic also to excite the opposition of all those who were friends to paper money. The people of property would be sure to be on the side of the plan, and it was impolitic to purchase their further attachment with the loss of the opposite class of Citizens

Mr. ELSEWORTH thought this a favorable moment to shut and bar the door against paper money. The mischiefs of the various experiments which had been made, were now fresh in the public mind and had excited the disgust of all the respectable part of

America. By withholding the power from the new Government more friends of influence would be gained to it than by almost any thing else. Paper money can in no case be necessary. Give the Government credit, and other resources will offer. The power may do harm, never good.

Mr. **RANDOLPH**, notwithstanding his antipathy to paper money, could not agree to strike out the words, as he could not foresee all the occasions which 21 might arise.

Mr. **WILSON**. It will have a most salutary influence on the credit of the United States to remove the possibility of paper money. This expedient can never succeed whilst its mischiefs are remembered, and as long as it can be resorted to, it will be a bar to other resources.

Mr. **BUTLER**, remarked paper was a legal tender in no Country in Europe. He was urgent for disarming the Government of such a power.

Mr. **MASON** was still averse to tying the hands of the Legislature altogether. If there was no example in Europe as just remarked, it might be observed on the other side, there was none in which the Government was restrained on this head.

Mr. **READ**, thought the words, if not struck out, would be as alarming as the mark of the Beast in Revelations.

Mr. **LANGDON** had rather reject the whole plan than retain the three words "(and emit bills")

On the motion for striking out

N. H. ay. Mas. ay. Ct ay. N. J. no. Pa. ay. Del. ay. Md. no. Va. ay. N. C. ay. S. C. ay. Geo. ay.

Each state had one vote. The Motion to strike the words "and emit bills" was agreed to by a vote of 9 to 2.

The language in Article I, Section 10 was debated and voted on August 28, 1787. Here again, is Madison's journal:

Art: XII.8 being 12 taken up.

MR. WILSON & **MR. SHERMAN** moved to insert after the words "coin money" the words "nor emit bills of credit, nor make any thing but gold & silver coin a tender in payment of debts" making these prohibitions absolute, instead of making the measures allowable (as in the XIII art:) with the consent of the Legislature of the U. S.

MR. GHORUM_thought the purpose would be as well secured by the provision of art: XIII which makes the consent of the Genl Legislature necessary, and in mode, no opposition would be excited; whereas an absolute prohibition of paper money would rouse the most desperate opposition from its partizans.

MR. SHERMAN thought this a favorable crisis for crushing paper money. If the consent of the Legislature could authorise emissions of it, the friends of paper money, would make every exertion to get into the Legislature in order to licence it.

The question being divided; on the 1st. part-"nor emit bills of credit"

N. H. ay. Mas. ay. Ct. ay. Pa. ay. Del. ay. Md. divd. Va. no. N. C. ay. S. C. ay. Geo. ay.

The prohibition against paper money was now absolute. The federal government was prohibited from emitting bills of credit, or paper money, in Article I, Section 8. The states were prohibited in Article I, Section 10 from making anything except gold and silver coin a tender in payment of debts.

The word tender, in this context means to offer. Nothing other than gold or silver was to be legally offered by the state governments to be used as money. Our constitution was ratified just over a year later on September 17, 1789. Congress adopted our first coinage act on April 2, 1792.

Our monetary system was to abandon the British system of pence, shillings, pounds, crowns, and guineas, in favor of a decimal system providing for the monetary unit to be called the dollar. The coinage act specified the weight of gold or silver in each dollar, and also provided for coins to be minted which were fractions of a dollar, dimes, quarters and half dollars. There was also provision for one, five, ten and twenty dollar coins.

Just a few years before the adoption of our constitution the Continental Currency had depreciated to the point it took $100 of paper currency to buy $1 of gold, at which time the Continental Currency was essentially worthless and ceased to circulate as money.

Commerce and industry were at a standstill and our economy was in a deplorable condition. Then, just a few years after the adoption of our constitution and the first Currency Act, George Washington was writing to friends abroad of the wonderful condition of our economy and the bright prospects for our young nation.

Do you as a supporter of the tea party movement want to see the economy of the United States once more on a sound footing and growing quickly? The solution is the same today as it was in August of 1787, all we must do is demand currency reform that replaces paper Federal Reserve Notes with circulating *gold* and *silver coinage.*

For the next 71 years, *gold* and *silver coins* circulated as *money.* State chartered banks issued bank notes, usually backed by fractional reserves, consisting mostly of state issued bonds, some of which were much better than others.

What is *fractional reserve* banking? Basically, it is a way to spend more money than you actually have - or lend it out at interest - and, hopefully not get caught. Here is how it works. A thousand years ago, before there were any banks in the modern sense, goldsmiths would hold gold for customers and issue receipts for the *gold.*

These paper receipts were much easier to carry around than the actual *gold.* Customers began to trade these receipts to merchants for products instead of buying things with *gold coins.* The merchant, now the holder of the receipt, could redeem it for the *gold.* It became more likely he too would simply give the *gold* receipt to another vendor for goods or services rather than cashing it in with the goldsmith.

These receipts for *gold*, on deposit with the goldsmith, were serving the function of *gold coins* in commerce. In effect, they had become a paper substitute for *money.* Suppose 1,000 people each deposited some *gold coins* with the goldsmith, taking receipts for their *gold.* These thousand paper receipts were now circulating in commerce, serving the purpose of *money.*

In the beginning, the goldsmith would have all the *gold* in his vault necessary to cash all the receipts if all the receipts were presented at the same time. That made the paper receipts backed by 100% *gold* reserves, as well as being redeemable on demand. Under such circumstances, these receipts were literally *good as gold* and passed as *money.*

An astute goldsmith made two observations. First, the paper receipts he printed and signed were being accepted in commerce as if they were *gold coins*! Second about 95% of the *gold* on deposit in his vault on any given day went unclaimed because only about 5% of the receipts were actually being redeemed for *gold coins*. Under these circumstances, it would be very easy for the goldsmith to just start writing receipts for *gold* that did not exist, and spending those receipts as if the receipts themselves were *gold coins*.

The goldsmith kept just enough actual *gold coins* in his vault to redeem the few receipts that were turned in on any given day. The effect of this was all the receipts in circulation were no longer backed by 100% reserves, but only a fraction of 100%, thus a *fractional reserve*. The written contract on the *gold* receipt might still promise the holder the ability to redeem the receipt for *gold* on demand.

However, the reality was, there is not enough *gold* in the goldsmith's vault to redeem more than a small fraction of the receipts in circulation. Perhaps the goldsmith had prudently kept 10% or even 15% of thetotal amount of *gold* all the receipts promised could be delivered. As long as the public had confidence in his receipts there were only about 5% of them actually being redeemed.

When something happened to shake the public confidence in the goldsmith, people went into a panic and decided to redeem the receipts for *gold*. This was the proverbial *run on the bank* in modern parlance. When the goldsmith could not pay a depositor in *gold* he was out of business, and possibly surrounded by angry receipt holders carrying a rope.

Suppose the goldsmith could persuade another goldsmith in town, or in another town, to lend him some *gold coins* so he could redeem any receipt as it was presented? In that case, the holders of receipts had restored confidence in the promises to pay in *gold* written on the receipts, and were once more willing to hold them and use them in commerce as if they were *money*.

The goldsmith also found another way to create an additional profit stream for his business. He could lend *money* for interest. The goldsmith did not want to actually loan borrowers *gold coins*. He loaned them paper receipts for *gold* which did not exist. The goldsmith did not care if he was repaid in *gold coins*, or in paper receipts for *gold*. When he was repaid in *gold coins*, his reserves increased, making his operation more secure. When he was repaid in paper receipts, more paper receipts were removed from circulation than he had loaned in the first place. Once again, this made his operation more secure.

Anything the goldsmith received was pure profit because the only thing he had loaned in the first place was paper receipts he had printed at no real cost other than paper and ink.

When the goldsmith loaned paper receipts for *gold* that did not exist, he wanted collateral for the loan. Collateral which did exist. Borrow from the goldsmith to buy real estate, pledging the real estate as collateral. Default on the loan, and the goldsmith could foreclose the real estate. The goldsmith gained something valuable, real estate, in exchange for something which had little real value in the first place, a receipt backed only by a *fractional reserve.*

When all this was a secret, known by only one goldsmith, if he was a prudent and careful man, he could amass great wealth, as long as he was never caught. Inevitably many goldsmiths each discovered the ability to do this. Do you want even greater safety and security if you are a goldsmith? Take the King in as a partner, and have him protect your fraudulent activities!

How does a businessman convince a King to participate in a fraudulent scheme? Simple, promise to *loan money* to the Crown! Most Kings were always interested in either building bigger castles, or fighting wars in foreign lands. Thus Mayer Amschel Rothschild (1744-1812) famously remarked *"permit me to issue and control the money of a nation, and I care not who makes its laws."*

You might think honest governments would pass laws to prohibit *fractional reserves* because they obviously must always be based upon the fraud of lending things purporting to have value, paper substitutes for *money*; which in reality have no value other than public *confidence* in the fraudsters.

The Kings and goldsmiths understood this system only worked as long as the people retained *confidence* in the value of the paper receipts for *gold coin.* Thus the Kings and goldsmiths knew themselves to be nothing more than *con* men. *Confidence* in the paper would *con* the people out of *gold*, goods, and land.

In reality, Kings generally cared a lot more about financing war and conquest, than in protecting their own citizens from the fraud of the goldsmiths. Rather than blow the whistle on these practices, governments decided to *regulate* how they were operated.

In modern times the law actually specified how much capital a bank must have and what reserve it must retain. Here in America honest money, that is *gold* and *silver coin,* circulated for the 71 years between the enactment of our first Coinage Act in 1792 and Mr. Lincoln's unconstitutional Greenbacks in 1863. State chartered banks were allowed to issue banknotes, paper substitutes for real *money*, and do so with reserves consisting of state issued bonds, themselves of dubious value.

People like the convenience of paper substitutes for real *money*. They also like the easy availability of credit and the ability to borrow. Businessmen like all the commerce that takes place when everyone has easy access to borrowed money. As business booms, more jobs are created making and selling all the things that are going to be purchased with borrowed paper substitutes for *money*.

The unholy alliance of politicians and bankers, the modern goldsmiths, always has a vested interest in constantly increasing the volume of paper substitutes for *money* in circulation. They convince themselves that the paper they issue magically becomes valuable just because people are willing to accept it and no reserve is even necessary. This is exactly like saying hot checks are OK as long as you can pass them.

Once you can create political patronage jobs, finance public works, fund foreign wars, and have a booming economy, all without having to raise taxes to pay the piper, there is a built in incentive to just keep printing more and more paper substitutes for *money*.

The public is both greedy and gullible; but they are not completely stupid. As the supply of paper substitutes for *money* increases, folks know sooner or later, the bubble will always burst. It has always burst, and it always will. Therefore reluctance to accept the paper substitutes for *money* sets in. In the beginning, people do not merely refuse to accept the paper substitutes and demand real *money - gold coin*. They simply start to create a two-tier price for goods and services.

There is some risk banknotes will be defaulted on and become worthless. Therefore my price for my goods and services must reflect I am assuming some of risk. I will offer a 10% discount for folks paying cash, *gold coin*, over folks paying with paper promissory notes of a bank.

As the volume of those notes continues to increase, the risk of default also increases. We are getting closer to the inevitable day of reckoning, on which nobody is going to want to be holding paper banknotes. Therefore, I now offer a 50% discount to people paying *gold,* over the price in paper notes. Eventually I am offering a 99% discount for *gold.* That is to say $1 in *gold* will buy as much as $100 in paper notes. At around 100:1 we have historically seen the paper notes stop circulating completely and everyone reverts to demanding cash money, that is *gold coins,* or bartered commodities, which have intrinsic value which banknotes lack.

When this happens to the notes from only one bank, there has been a *run* on that bank. The economy continues to inflate based upon all the other paper substitutes for *money* still circulating. When the collapse is system wide and the public demands cash, i.e. *gold,* instead of banknotes, there is said to be an economic panic.

Prior to 1863 only state chartered banks issued notes. Most of these circulated, always at some discount against *coined money,* and eventually the bank failed making its notes worthless. Anyone holding those notes as if they were *money* got wiped out. Most state chartered banks went broke in about five years.

Abraham Lincoln was a Whig for most of his life, becoming a Republican nine years before he died. The Whig party had three major tenets; they supported central banking and paper substitutes for *money,* they believed in *internal improvements,* and they supported high protective tariffs. By *internal improvements,* they meant taxpayer funded public works. Many of the railroads and public works the government subsidized in the 19th century were about as economically sound as solar panel manufacturer Solyndra is today.

As president, Mr. Lincoln was able to have Congress pass a Legal Tender Act in 1862 and issue *Greenback* currency in 1863. The new notes were called *Greenbacks* because one side of the note was printed in green ink and the other side in black ink, a practice continues to this day with paper substitutes for money.

These notes were clearly an unconstitutional scheme. However, Lincoln had already tried and failed to do what the constitution authorized and *"borrow Money upon the credit of the United States."* The New York banking firms willing to lend real *money, gold coin,* to the Lincoln regime wanted to charge interest ranging from 24% to as much as 36% which Lincoln was clearly unwilling to pay.

He would not have been able to borrow enough *money* to finance the Union armies at any rate of interest. Lincoln's solution was to simply have congress pass Legal Tender Acts under the pretense they were constitutional exercises of the authority to raise and support an army and a navy.

A Legal Tender Act is nothing more than a law requiring the public to accept the paper notes as if they were money even though there are no reserves and the notes are not redeemable in specie. The Legal Tender Act of 1862 made two exceptions to the Legal Tender status of the unbacked *Greenbacks,* they could not be used to pay import tariffs, and, the government could not use *Greenbacks* to pay the interest due on US Government bonds.

The reason for these two exceptions was very simple. First, over half of the government's income at that time was derived from the tariff on imports. By requiring this to continue to be paid in *gold coin*, the government took in enough *gold* to pay the interest on its bonds in *gold*. Second, if the government had paid the interest on its bonds with *Greenbacks* instead of *gold*, it would have became impossible to sell government bonds.

The initial issue of *Greenbacks* was $150,000,000 worth. The government just printed them like monopoly money and spent them into circulation to pay for the expenses of the Union Army.

In spite of the Legal Tender Acts, these notes never circulated on par with *gold coin*, or even with other banknotes redeemable in *gold* on demand. As the war progressed, additional issues of *Greenbacks* were printed and issued into circulation. This, in turn, drove down the purchasing power of these notes even more. By the end of 1864 a *Greenback* only bought about 35% of what a gold dollar would purchase.

Many writers have stated - incorrectly - the Greenbacks and the equally worthless paper currency of the Confederacy rose and fell based upon which Army was winning on the battlefield at the time. In reality, the decline in purchasing power of both Union and Confederate notes was based upon the numbers of those notes in circulation. Larger numbers of notes in circulation directly caused the decline in the purchasing power of the notes.

After the war, the purchasing power of the *Greenbacks* continued to decline sharply until, eventually, they stopped circulating as *money* and were only purchased by speculators at rates as low as 500:1 or even 1,000:1. Once speculators had purchased most of these *Greenbacks*, many of the speculators foreign central banks, the friends of paper money began political agitation to make the *Greenbacks,* known officially as United States Notes, redeemable for the full face value in *gold*. This law was passed in 1875 and went into effect in 1879.

Needless to say, if the notes were redeemable, at their full face value in *gold,* the purchasing power went back up. By 1879 when they were redeemable in *gold,* they once more circulated with purchasing power 100% of the face value.

During the war Mr. Lincoln wanted to drive the notes issued by state banks out of circulation and force the acceptance of his *Greenbacks.* The National Banking Act of 1863 was passed, placing a 10% tax on the notes issued by state chartered banks. Naturally, this had the desired effect of driving all state bank notes out of circulation and forcing all state banks to apply for a national charter, and use United States Notes, or go out of business.

These measures were blatantly unconstitutional, and had the effect of robbing the poor farmers and others who were paid in United States Notes for supplying the Union Army. It was possible to pass such measures through congress only because the Southern members, all Democrats, were no longer seated in Congress. The Republicans were now able to adopt all the old proposals of the defunct Whig party; a high tariff, paper substitutes for *money,* centralization of banking and currency, and massive *internal improvements,* what we call public works today.

After the War Between the States, the National Banks continued the practice of fractional reserve banking and were allowed to issue National Bank Notes, using federal government bonds as collateral reserve. The results of these experiments with paper substitutes for *money* were no better than had been achieved before the war by state chartered banks.

National Bank Notes still circulated, often at steep discounts, compared to *gold dollars.* National Banks still went broke every five years on the average.

The bankers and friends of paper money continued to agitate for another central bank. This was accomplished in 1913 with passage of the Federal Reserve Act. The United States now had a monetary system consisted of:

- Circulating *gold coins*
- Circulating *silver coins*
- United States Notes (Greenbacks)
- National Bank Notes
- Silver Certificates
- Gold certificates
- Federal Reserve Notes.

All seven of which circulated at their face value and were colloquially referred to as *dollars*.

There was a lot more *silver coinage* in circulation than *gold* mainly because *gold* was minted in larger denominations. There were *gold* coins minted for $1, $3, $5, $10, $20, and $50, with ten and twenty dollar denominations, known as Eagles and Double Eagles, being the most common.

Silver coinage was minted in 3¢, 10¢, 25¢, and 50¢ denominations as well as silver dollars. Silver and gold certificates and other paper notes circulated at face value because they were readily redeemable in *silver* or *gold*. After 1933 FDR got a law passed to stop the circulation of gold coins and the mint melted down gold coins dated 1933 and they were never issued into circulation. It is believed 12 of the 1933 Double Eagles, or Twenty Dollar Gold Pieces, were smuggled out of the mint instead of being melted. Nine of these were recently confiscated from the estate of a deceased collector when his heirs sent them to the Mint for verification of their authenticity.

Silver coins continued to be minted and issued into circulation through the end of 1964. Beginning in 1965, dimes and quarters were nickel-clad copper with no *silver* in them. The Half Dollar coin continued to have 40% *silver* content until 1970 when it too became a nickel-clad copper slug. The next year Dollar coins, bearing the image of former President Eisenhower, were also struck for circulation as nickel-clad copper slugs. These were popular for a time in Las Vegas slot machines but neither the Half Dollar nor the Dollar coins circulated much after 1965.

Silver Certificates and Gold Certificates were retired from circulation. United States Notes continued to circulate but only in the $5 denomination. Federal Reserve Notes (FRN) were re-designed to remove the promise to redeem them on demand for lawful *money*, meaning *silver or gold coin*.

Once more there was no impediment to artificially increasing the supply of these paper substitutes for real constitutional *money*. Since merchants could no longer give two prices, one in *gold* and one in paper notes, because *gold* and *silver* no longer circulated, they simply began to inflate the price as paid in *paper money* as FRN came to be erroneously called. In 1964, a gallon of regular gasoline sold for 18¢. Gasoline is not more expensive than it was in 1964; the purchasing power of the paper *dollar* has declined dramatically.

Everyone in America understands the purchasing power of the dollar has declined and prices have risen correspondingly. Many people understand the Federal Reserve Act gave the Federal Reserve Bank the power to buy US Government Bonds with FRN that are printed at no cost. Most people know some sort of currency reform is necessary.

The friends of paper money work constantly, as they have done since before our constitution was written, to preserve what Judge Roger Sherman said was a *"pernicious evil"* in his 1752 book, *Caveat Against Injustice*. Judge Sherman, from Connecticut, was the only man to sign the Articles of Confederation, Declaration of Independence and the US Constitution. Roger Sherman, a Superior Court Judge for 22 years was the author of the words in Article I, Section 10, of the US Constitution *"No state shall make anything except gold or silver coin a tender in payment of debt."* President Thomas Jefferson once remarked, *"Roger Sherman was a man who never said a foolish thing in his life."*

Today the friends of paper money are still slithering among us, still spreading the Devil's lie that an *elastic* medium of exchange causes economic prosperity. This makes about as much sense as saying rubber rulers are more accurate for measuring distances because they give you the freedom to make inches any size you want them.

The modern version of the evil scheme to preserve paper *money* is to distract the public by pointing out, correctly, the Federal Reserve charges interest on each note. The friends of paper *money* then assert, incorrectly, the solution is to have the Treasury issue unbacked United States Notes, which bear no interest.

Think about this, friends of paper money are telling us it is better to move the power to issue unbacked paper substitutes for *money* from Ben S. Bernanke at the Federal Reserve to someone like Nancy Pelosi in congress. No, gentle reader, the problem definitely is not the interest on the notes. The only problem is the notes are unbacked by *gold* and regularly inflated by means of a process currently called *quantitative easing*.

You must be very clear. The problem with using paper notes as substitutes for *money* never has been, is not, and never will be, the interest collected by the parties issuing the notes. The evil inherent in all forms of unbacked paper notes is they can, and will, be inflated, driving up prices. Unbacked United States Notes that do not have a 100% reserve, and are not convertible on demand to *gold or silver*, will not stop price inflation, and the eventual destruction of our republic. An *elastic* currency, must, by definition, always be a fraudulent currency. Period.

Chapter Thirteen
The Bible & the Constitution

This book, like the tea party movement itself, is very critical of the many excesses and failures of the federal government of the United States. We have loudly protested corruption, waste, fraud, debt, other excesses of every description, and the taxes necessary to support these evils.

From time to time we have been chastised by well meaning, but seriously misguided, Christian brethren and Clergy, for our protests against the evils of the federal government. Most often they cite the opening verses of Romans, Chapter 13, where Paul, writing to the Romans, begins *"Let every soul be subject to the governing authorities. For there is no authority except from God, and the authorities that exist are appointed by God."*

Why are these brethren misguided? They make a fundamental mistake by assuming the federal government of the United States is the governing authority over we the people. In reality, the federal government is not any authority over you or I. The federal government is, instead, the servant of our servants. Allow me to explain.

Thomas Jefferson wrote in the Declaration of Independence *all men are created equal, and are endowed by their Creator with certain unalienable rights.* Therefore, when Romans, Chapter 13 says *there is no authority except from God,* it must necessarily include the authority vested in those *unalienable rights* Jefferson referenced in the Declaration of Independence.

This incredible insight and understanding made the American Revolution of 1776 completely different from any revolution before it in the whole history of the world. This was the first time men recognized the source of all of the rights, powers, or immunities, they enjoyed was not the government, nor do our rights come from the head of state. Our rights were endowed by our *Creator!* Among those rights Jefferson specifically mentioned life, liberty, and property.

Heavily influenced by the great English philosopher John Locke, Jefferson understood there were natural laws, made by the *Creator,* which were superior to any laws made by man. Jefferson's idea, considered radical at the time, understood the source of all rights was the *Creator,* not the government, and not the King. In effect, every may was sovereign over himself. Louisiana's Governor Huey P. Long once observed in America *"Every man is a King. Every woman is a Queen. Every home is a castle!"*

The American Revolution was first preached from the pulpits of our Churches, and the refrain heard everywhere was *no King but Jesus.*

When I first put on the uniform of our country and took the oath to preserve, protect, and defend, the constitution of the United States, I was introduced to something called the Chain-of-Command.

Privates, as I was, were subject to following the orders of Corporals. Corporals, in turn, were under the authority of Sergeants. Sergeants, of which there were several classes, were subject to following the orders of officers. The same was true in the officer ranks starting with the lowly Second Lieutenants, and progressing through First Lieutenants, Captains, Majors, Lieutenant Colonels, Colonels, to the Generals, of which there were five levels. This process continued with even the Generals being subject to the Secretary of the Army, who answered to the Secretary of Defense. The Secretary of Defense answered to the president, who obeyed laws passed by congress. Finally, congress, through the electoral process, is subject to the will of the voters. Folks just like you.

Our Founding Fathers were the first revolutionaries in history to establish a correct Chain-of-Command. They started at the top, with the ultimate authority, the Creator of this universe. Chain-of-Command, still in effect today, goes like this:

God created man, and, necessarily, the Creator rules over the creatures. All of our rights, privileges, and immunities, flow from our Creator. All of our duties, responsibilities, and allegiance, flow back to our Creator.

Men created each of the state governments. They did so by delegating some, but not all, of the rights given to them by the *Creator* of the universe. Applying the same principles as in the paragraph above, men rule over the governments they create. In our American system, all of the powers of the State governments are given to them by the consent of the governed. That means the government's power comes from we the people.

The representatives of the States met in Philadelphia in 1787 to create the federal government. The radical ideal, embodied as the fundamental principle of our government, was the federal government is a government of few, limited, and defined, powers delegated to it by the States. All powers not so delegated, are retained by the states, or by the people, respectively.

Therefore, the state government was created by my ancestors to serve as their servant. The representatives of *our servant the state government*, in turn, created the federal government to be the servant of the states. The federal government of the United States is, therefore, the servant of my servant! I will be judged, by my *Creator*, for how well, or poorly, I supervise my servants on this earth.

Let every soul be subject to the governing authorities... [Romans 13:1] in the United States of America, the governing authorities are we the people!

This is important. I am the authority over the federal government of the United States... and so are you!

In England, as in much of the rest of the world, the King was the sovereign. Only here in the United States has the sovereignty been vested in the people themselves. The United States Supreme Court in the case of <u>United States v. George Washington Custis Lee, 106 US 196 (1882)</u> stated the following as part of the majority opinion:
Volume 106 U. S. at Pages 208-209

Under our system, the people, who are there [in England] called subjects, are the sovereign. Their rights, whether collective or individual, are not bound to give way to a sentiment of loyalty to the person of the monarch. The citizen here knows no person, however near to those in power or however powerful himself, to whom he need yield the rights which the law secures to him when it is well administered. When he, in one of the courts of competent jurisdiction, has established his right to property, [p.209] there is no reason why deference to any person, natural or artificial, not even the United States, should prevent him from using the means which the law gives him for the protection and enforcement of right.

This case had its origins in the War Between the States. Confederate Gen. Robert E. Lee's home at Arlington, Virginia was an inheritance of his wife Mary Custis Lee, the Great Granddaughter of Martha Washington. During the war, a portion of Virginia was occupied by the Union Army, meaning Gen. Lee's home was behind enemy lines.

In 1864 the Yankees passed a property tax law, which required homeowners to appear *in person* and pay a tax. Mary Custis Lee sent an agent to pay the tax of $92.07. The offer was refused because the homeowner was not paying in person, and the land was seized. This seizure was the real purpose of law.

Lee, a graduate of the US Military Academy at West Point, had been a Colonel in the US Army when the war started. He was widely considered to be the most capable officer in the Army. Abe Lincoln offered Lee command of the Union Army when the war started. Not wishing to bear arms against his native State, Lee resigned his commission instead. He was later appointed Commander of the Confederate Army of Northern Virginia.

Lee's brilliant leadership is universally acknowledged to have saved the Confederacy, for a time, and undoubtedly prolonged the war considerably. He was loved in the South and hated up North. In 1864, with Yankee casualties mounting, Union Army Quartermaster General, Montgomery C. Meigs ordered Union war dead buried in the front yard of Lee's ancestral home. This was done out of spite toward a hated enemy.

Upon the death of Robert E. Lee, his oldest son, George Washington Custis Lee, inherited the estate and in 1874 the younger Lee, sued the caretakers of the cemetery to have his home returned. He prevailed in the County Court in Virginia. The federal government removed the case to the federal Circuit Court and argued; among other things, George Washington Custis Lee could not sue the federal government based upon the government's claim of *sovereign immunity*.

The US government cited a long string of cases as precedent going back to a rule in England that the King could not be sued, in part because it would be absurd for the King to serve process upon himself and appear in his own court. The established rule was no subject could sue the King without his permission.

The case reached the United States Supreme Court in 1882. In a 5-4 decision, the United States Supreme Court ruled American citizens, including Lee, are not subjects of a sovereign as in England. The Court correctly pointed out, in this country there is no one office or person who embodies the sovereignty, in America the sovereignty resides in the whole body of the people.

Lee won his case, the estate at Arlington was returned to him. He then sold it to the federal government for the sum of $150,000 in gold which would be equal to more than $3 million in today's paper money, due to the depreciation in the purchasing power of our paper substitutes for dollars over the ensuing 129 years

Today the dead from every American war, including Iraq and Afghanistan, are buried at what is now Arlington National Cemetery, including three tombs of unknown soldiers from both World Wars and Vietnam.

The supreme authority over the government - the sovereignty - in the United States of America is not vested in the President. We have no King. There is not one person, or one office that exercises the sovereignty over our nation. Sovereign authority rests with the entire body of the American people. You and I are the sovereigns appointed by God to rule over this nation.

Sovereign authority is the real strength of the *tea party* movement. We may indeed effect elections and help choose the next president. However, our real power and authority are already being exercised by all of us collectively. My Christian brethren who misunderstand Romans, Chapter Thirteen, have forgotten the words of the Prophet Samuel.

We read in the Eighth Chapter of First Samuel the people of Israel wanted to have a King to rule over them and fight their battles for them *like all the nations.* [Verse 5] Samuel was concerned the people were rejecting him, and prayed to God about it. God told Samuel *they have not rejected you, but they have rejected me* [Verse 7]

God told Samuel to give the people a King like all the other nations but to solemnly forewarn them, and show them the behavior of the King who will reign over them. [Verse9]

We read [Verses 11-18] *And he said, "This will be the behavior of the King who will reign over you: he will take your sons and appoint them for his own chariots and to be his horsemen, and some will run before his chariots.*

He will appoint captains over his thousands and captains over his fifties, will set some to plow his ground and reap his harvest, and some to make weapons of war and equipment for his chariots.

"He will take your daughters to be perfumers, cooks, and bakers.

"And he will take the best of your fields, your vineyards, and your olive groves, and give them to his servants.

"He will take a tenth of your grain and your vintage, and give it to his officers and servants.

"And he will take your male servants, and your female servants, your finest young men, and your donkeys, and put them to his work.

"He will take a tenth of your sheep. And you will be his servants.

"And you will cry out in day because of your king whom you have chosen for yourselves, and the Lord will not hear you in day.

Once you truly understand both the Scriptures and American history, it is clear we are the sovereigns, and God has sometimes used big government as a way to punish people who have turned from following his ways.

Next time a Christian clergyman, citing Romans Thirteen, tells you to sit on your behind, sing loudly, and turn over all the troubles in the land to Jesus, while you do nothing about them; feel free to show him the rather substantial error of his ways!

Chapter Fourteen
Protest Movements Through History

Beginning in 2009, the *tea party* movement swept across this nation, fundamentally changing the political landscape. The movement raised awareness of the American people to the crisis caused by massive government spending, massive government deficits, and the oppressive tax burdens that have stagnated our economy. We saw the largest mass protest in the history of the world on September 12, 2009 and similar protests in thousands of large cities and small towns all across America. The protests of 2009 led in 2010 to a dramatic shift in power in the US House of Representatives with the election of 87 freshmen Republicans, almost all tea party supporters. Here in South Carolina, four of our six U.S. Representatives were replaced with tea party supported members.

There has been much speculation, particularly among its detractors, as to whether the tea party movement will have any lasting effect. Will the tea party movement continue to dominate the American political landscape as it clearly did in the 2010 mid-term elections? Will tea party reforms within the Republican Party become a permanent feature of the GOP? Or, as the left hopes, will this disorganized movement, with little structure, and no national leader, merely be a flash in the pan?

Some historic events made a short impact on the national scene, then faded away to become nothing more than a footnote in our history books. Anti-Immigrant, anti-Masonic, abolitionists, Prohibition, and numerous other minor political parties serve as examples of such flash-in-the-pan movements.

Other social movements fundamentally altered the fabric of our nation, permanently changing American culture in the process. In the last century in particular, there were two great social movements with lasting impacts on the nation. Political impacts which continue to this day. The most lasting were *organized labor,* and the so-called *civil rights* movement.

It is beneficial to look into the life cycle of such movements.

They followed a seven-stage life cycle, a pattern the *tea party* movement appears to be following thus far. This author is reasonably convinced of the permanence of the *tea party* movement, at least in some form, because of the serious debt crisis that spawned the movement, and the millions of people from all walks of life who embraced the movement in order to right those fundamental wrongs.

The *tea party* movement certainly has the potential to become far more prominent in American political culture than either *organized labor*, or *civil rights*, hopefully without the excesses, violence, and abuses, that characterized, and detracted from the impact of, those earlier social movements.

Let's examine the seven stages in the life of a social movement. We will look at *labor, civil rights*, and the *tea party* to illustrate those seven stages.

INJUSTICE OR CRISIS:

Stage one. Every great movement is born due to some terrible problem, which eventually reaches a crisis.

In the case of *organized labor*, working conditions in the United States in the latter portion of the 19th century and the early 20th century were, nothing short of deplorable. Safety took a back seat to production. Operators of coalmines coldly calculated so many miners were going to be killed in mining accidents for X number of tons of coal being produced. It was easier, and cheaper, to hire more miners to replace those killed, than to invest in available technology that would have made the mines safer.

Industrial concerns, particularly textile manufacturing, employed large numbers of unskilled workers including many children, some as young as age nine. They worked 14 and 16-hour days, often six days a week. Not only did children go to work at a very young age and work long hours; they were subjected to unsafe conditions. These included conditions that maimed, killed, and destroyed health.

In the case of *civil rights*, the Black population of this country was subjected to social discrimination. Prior to the 1960's Black folks were often denied the equal protection of the laws to which they were supposed to be entitled. Almost a hundred years after the abolition of chattel slavery, the descendants of former slaves were still not afforded the same legal protection as all other citizens. The long history of race relations in America is beyond the scope of this chapter but every reasonable person would agree Black folks in the 1950's and earlier, had not enjoyed the same legal protection as white people, particularly here in the South.

In the case of the *tea party* movement, our people have suffered a long, terrible, economic decline in this nation that has been either caused, or exacerbated, by the actions of the federal government of the United States. Today the federal government is a massive, bloated, wasteful, and corrupt monster that sucks the economic life out of the productive sector, and destroys the possibility of the American dream, for tens of millions of our citizens.

Jobs have been exported overseas. Millions of illegal aliens have invaded our nation and brazenly demand *"rights"* to our welfare system. That welfare system has grown to a bloated monster that deprived generations of the poor of any opportunity to improve their station in life. Criminals roam our cities, protestors burn our flag, and terrorists threaten our safety. Energy costs skyrocket as we buy oil from our enemies, the Federal Reserve further debases our currency, our people sink into debt, and our government must subsist on money borrowed from our sworn enemies in red China. Unemployment, officially at 9.1% actually approaches 50% among the young and in some minority communities.

Thus, in the beginning of all three social movements, *labor, civil rights*, and the *tea parties*, there were terrible problems, national in scope, which reached crisis proportions. Victims finally get mad as hell and say we are not going to take it any more.

PROTEST AND REVOLT:

Stage two in the development of a lasting social movement is *protest and revolt*. In all three cases, the legal and political institutions that were supposed to provide redress of grievances failed to produce needed relief. In all three cases, *labor, civil rights,* and the *tea parties*, millions of people poured into the streets. They were convinced the system was broken, and there was no other hope of fixing the problem except taking matters into their own hands. In the cases of *labor and civil rights*, those protests turned violent with people being killed and millions of dollars worth of property being damaged. At least so far, this has not happened with the *tea party* movement.

A few *tea party* people hinted at violence by carrying signs reading *"If the first amendment does not work; try the second amendment"* but there has been no actual violence. To their credit, the participants in the *tea party* movement have understood violence, terrorism, murder, rioting, and widespread destruction of private property that characterized the early days of the *labor* and the *civil rights* movements, turned off many reasonable Americans who would have shown sympathy for the legitimate concerns of workers and Black people in the absence of the violence.

The *tea party* movement has remained homogenous and focused on economic reform and individual freedom issues. In contrast both the *labor* and the *civil rights* movements were heavily infiltrated from the beginning with communists whose real goal was never to just improve the lot of the working class or the Black people but to foment violent revolution as a way to weaken America. Both labor and civil rights were characterized by rioting, destruction of property, and widespread lawbreaking. Nor do I refer to some simple, but unjust law requiring a person to ride on the back of the bus. I am talking about murdering police, widespread looting, rape, drug abuse, public promiscuity, bombings and arson.

The American people have always been reasonable, moderate, temperate and hard working. An appeal to basic fairness, or a complaint about blatant unfairness will garner broad support. We tend to be generous, charitable, gregarious, and optimistic, as a nation. The American dream has always been to live reasonably free and be able to work hard, so you can become anything you have the ability to achieve.

Americans are willing to root for the underdog as long as he is working hard to help himself. We are willing to listen to reasonable complaints and demand justice and fairness. All we ask in return is you speak English, work hard, obey the law, and respect your neighbor's rights and his property. We don't like anyone being picked on, exploited, or treated unfairly. Neither do we want any class, group, race, religion or other classification to have any special place in society or be given privileges the rest of us do not enjoy.

Americans tend to make a great distinction between civil disobedience and street crime. When someone refused military conscription due to sincerely held religious beliefs, Americans wanted some accommodation made for them to be able to serve in some manner that did not conflict with their religious convictions. After all, this nation was founded, at least in part, by folks leaving places in Europe where they were not allowed to worship God

158

according to the dictates of their conscience.

In contrast, a person who joined a communist anti-war movement and planted bombs that blew up Army recruiting offices and killed recruiters gained no support whatsoever for his or her cause. In fact, there was a backlash demanding better law enforcement as the public rallied around the patriotic recruiters, and prayed for their families.

MULTIPLE ORGANIZATIONS:

Stage three. Sooner or later, protests designed to raise public awareness of a problem, give way to formal organizations that propose solutions to the problem.

In the case of the *labor* and the *civil rights* movements it took many years for those in the movement to go from protesting and random violence, to the stage where they created formal organizations to advocate for thier agenda.

There are many factors that contributed to this being a decades long effort. Three major reasons stand out:

1. Both the *labor,* and the *civil rights* movements were heavily infiltrated by communists who always urged violence, while claiming the American system was fundamentally flawed and should be overthrown completely.

2. Communications in the late nineteenth and early twentieth centuries was much less developed than it is today. Early *labor* and *civil rights* leaders did not have the Internet for Facebook, Twitter, Blogs, and online research. Neither did they have smart phones, laptop computers, iPhones, iPads, and all the other methods of low cost instantaneous communications.

3. Participants in these movements tended to be mostly from the lowest economic and social groups in the country. Most of them, as a result, had very little money, education, or political influence.

In contrast the *tea party* movement pulls its supporters almost exclusively from the middle class. Middle class Americans today are more likely to be college educated, gainfully employed and homeowners. The *tea party* movement was a true grassroots rising of the people, the Hundredth Monkey Syndrome. As with any movement comprising almost 1/5 of the population of the United States, there is some minor bickering and a few egos have clashed. By and large, the goals of the *tea party* movement are mainstream conservative values and principles.

While a vocal minority of *tea partiers are* critical of the GOP, it is fair to say the *tea party* goals are summarized rather nicely in the platform of the Republican Party. In fact, one of the criticisms leveled by the *tea party*, with some merit, is the GOP establishment has not always been vigorous enough in promoting the fine ideals embodied in the GOP platform.

In the third stage of a political movement, permanent organizations begin to appear. These may be small *labor unions* in local businesses, various *"Negro"* organizations beginning with the NAACP in 1907, or local *Tea Parties* in every town of any size across America.

No movement has ever been represented by any single organization empowered to speak for everyone in movement. When we examine the *civil rights* movement, particularly in the 1960's, we find militant communist revolutionary organizations, radical Moslem organizations, relatively mainstream Christian organizations, and groups promoting Black education, and Black business and commercial interests.

The focus and goals ranged from pleas to emulate the white man and learn to be successful by copying his work ethic at one end of the spectrum; to hate whitey, as you loot, rob, rape and burn baby burn, on the other extreme. Almost all organizations and participants wanted honest equality of opportunity and the equal protection of the law.

Others demanded handouts and special privileges, preached hatred of white people, and embraced separatist movements as diverse as Black Power, the creation of a *"Negro Soviet Republic"* in five Southern states, or the creation of the *Nation of Islam.*

As the number of *civil rights* organizations increased, they also learned how to extort huge sums of money from corporate America. While the Black population as a group was rather poor, there were plenty of other sources of funding. There were plenty of very wealthy white folks, mostly guilt ridden liberal celebrities, ready to contribute huge sums of money. Other money was extorted from businesses large and small. They were threatened with, usually false accusations of racism, along with boycotts, demonstrations, frivolous lawsuits, and destruction of property if they did not cough up payoff money. Most Fortune 500 companies paid up and many of them continue to pay to this day. The Mafia has never had a shakedown artist as skillful, vicious, or effective as the *"Reverend"*

Jessie Jackson, to cite but one of many examples.

There are huge foundation grants from the Ford, Rockefeller, and other left of center foundations. Churches, and not just Baptists, have never been bashful about passing the hat at every opportunity. To their credit, many of the faith based organizations, while embracing some of the radical left ideas, have also provided numerous social programs that mentor youth, feed the hungry, clothe the naked, and minister to the sick and the incarcerated in a true Christian manner.

The ultimate source of funding for the various causes of the Black people in America has been the State and federal governments. Economists call these funds *transfer pay*ments. That means the money is being taken from the folks who produce it; and given to folks who produce nothing. The fact is most of the folks paying are white, and many of the folks being paid are not white.

Certainly, there have always been a handful of white trash on welfare, but they are a small part of the overall culture of entitlement. Unfortunately, the *white trash on welfare* demographic is increasing in this country, particularly among young people and substance abusers. Government wealth re-distribution programs have never in history lifted up the downtrodden. They have always brought down the productive class to the lowest common denominator.

Like the *tea party* movement and the *civil rights* movement, *labor* too saw the creation of hundreds of *labor* related organizations. Both *organized labor* and the *tea p*arties were much more focused on a few core beliefs than the *civil rights* circus that has been all over the board. In both cases, those core issues tend to be primarily economic and financial in nature.

Labor organizations are, comprised of blue-collar workers who are middle class and gainfully employed. Like the *civil rights* movement, labor did have some legitimate complaints and laudable goals, particularly prior to 1938.

Organized labor complained of unsafe working conditions in dozens of industries all over the country. They made a good case many of those dangerous conditions existed because employers were too callous to bother with basic safety improvements that would have saved lives and prevented accidents and injuries. These are goals all fair-minded Americans can embrace.

Organized labor organizations worked hard for basic fairness in other areas as well. Many of the reforms they worked for over the fifty years before 1938 are things we take for granted today. *Labor* demanded and got, an end to child labor, an 8-hour day, overtime pay for longer hours, a 40-hour workweek, and a five-day workweek.

These are all reasonable goals most fair-minded Americans fully embrace. In fact, once these modern reforms were adopted, industrial workers actually had a much softer life than many Americans who were not covered by these gains. Farmers still worked from sunrise to sunset, often seven days a week, and many still do. The same is true for small business owners and other self-employed people who often work 12 hours a day or longer and usually six days a week.

Moving from fundamental fairness to *"what's in it for us?"* labor also demanded, under threat of extortion, higher pay, medical benefits, stock options, seats on corporation boards of directors, paid vacations, sick pay, medical insurance, maternity leaves, profit sharing, and educational opportunities among other things.

They negotiated long-term contracts, and very generous retirement packages. *Labor* has successfully demanded and gotten, work rules that in many cases allow union members to take over much of the middle management of businesses and specify what workers can and cannot be asked to do.

Vital to labor, and detrimental to the businesses, and to the public at large, *labor* has successfully demanded closed shops. Employers may not hire non-union workers on jobs covered by a union contract. In states without Right To Work laws, even non-union workers can be required to pay dues to unions.

On the good side, unions instituted apprenticeship programs for skilled crafts, usually four years in duration that were very successful in training young workers to become highly skilled craftsmen with a trade they may work at for life. The unions could usually point with pride to such journeyman craftsmen who graduated from a four year apprenticeship program and say they were better trained, more proficient, and more productive than non union journeymen in the same trades who did not complete any formal apprenticeship program.

The non-union craftsman was likely to have learned his skills by years of on-the-job training. In some cases, those craftsmen were every bit as qualified as union men or better, but in a lot of cases, they were minimally qualified.

Union craftsmen got jobs through the union's employment halls and were rigidly qualified for the positions they filled. Non-union workers obtained jobs responding to advertising, from state employment agencies, and as often as not, because they were recommended by a buddy, or hired by a family member or an in-law.

PUBLIC OUTRAGE AND SYMPATHY:

Stage four in the life cycle of any movement. The movement, having gone through the crisis that spawned it, the protest against crisis, the growth and maturity phase where multiple organizations spring up, is now able to tap into sympathy among the public at large.

Labor had legitimate complaints over the conditions of workers in America in the last quarter of the nineteenth century and the early twentieth century. These ranged from low wages to unsafe conditions and even, in extreme cases, death. Due to poorer means of education and communications, and to the fact labor organizations often embraced both communist ideals and violence that would make a Mafia Don blush, it took almost forty years before the average American began to see the need for reforms in labor and safety laws.

Once Clergymen, housewives, college students, and newspaper editors began to take up the cause of *labor* they were finally seen in a more favorable light. This was particularly true in certain geographic areas, and among Democrats. *Labor* would have arrived at this stage of public acceptance and indignation over real injustices decades earlier if they had not embraced radical un-American ideals and often resorted to violence.

The *civil rights* movement followed a similar pattern. The violence, crime and radical ideals infused and permeated the civil rights movement turning off many Americans and actually scared the hell out of quite a few folks. People in the South remembered the horrors of *Reconstruction*. People in the North, the Mid-west, and on the west coast, saw the rioting and crime in their cities.

Still, there was no denying the Black man had indeed been subjected to real discrimination and injustice. White America would no longer support laws prevented a man from voting, serving on a jury, eating in a public place, or being hired on any job he was well qualified for merely because of the color of his skin.

In many cases, the Black man, and particularly his leaders and organizations, could be their own worst enemy. White people wanted to embrace fundamental fairness and absolute equality. They were, however, turned off by demands for special privileges, and for laws that actually discriminate against white people. They could call it reparations, or affirmative action, or what ever the politically correct euphemism of the day might be - in plain fact, all these things are names for racial discrimination against white people.

Most of America did not ever want a qualified Black man passed over for a job or a promotion. Neither did they want a qualified white man passed over for a job or a promotion for which he was best qualified because some less qualified individual of a different race was going to be hired instead. Both were equally wrong, they were wrong for the same reason... they still are.

I have been asked my views on race many times. They are quite simple. Every one of us has different God given talents. If you want to deny equality, at the starting line in the contest of life, you are a *racist*, and I want nothing to do with you.

Every one of us is going to have different God given talents; and some of us will use those talents more fully than others. If you want to mandate equality of result at the finish line in the contest of life, you are a *communist*, and I want to have nothing to do with you either! That is about as clear as I can make it.

The *tea party* movement has reached the fourth stage of the life of a political movement; public acceptance and outrage at the problems we are fighting. In the case of *organized labor* it took about fifty years to reach the stage of public acceptance. With the *civil rights* movement, it took closer to seventy-five years to get there.

The *tea party* movement has managed to accomplish the same result in only three years. Some of the dramatic success of the tea party movement may be attributed to talk radio, FOX News, Facebook, Twitter, the Internet, smart phones, iPads, and all the other components of our modern communications system. Communications technology is only one small part of the phenomenal success of the *tea party* movement in gaining mainstream acceptance.

A bigger part of the rapid success of the *tea party* movement can be attributed to the fact the *tea party* has been focused like a laser beam on issues of fundamental economic fairness, has not been infiltrated by any radical un-American elements, and has not resorted to violence or intimidation. See **Appendix C** below to contrast the tea party movement with the Occupy Wall Street crowd. Any violence would have turned off people in middle America who are now generally supportive of the *tea party* movement and its common sense agenda of getting out of debt and putting America back to work.

LEGISLATIVE VICTORIES:

Stage five in the life of any movement is the attainment of legislative victories.

Over the last century *organized labor* won hundreds of legislative victories and court cases. The National Labor Relations Act of 1935, commonly known as the Wagoner Act, guaranteed the rights of workers to form unions, and of unions to represent all workers on a job whether they were union members or not. The Act also created the National Labor Relations Board (NLRB) to resolve labor disputes. *The National Labor Relations Act* was amended in 1947 by the *Taft-Hartley Act* that corrected some of the excesses of the original legislation in favor of unions. Among other things *Taft-Hartley* protected the rights of workers to refuse to join unions if they chose not to.

The *Fair Labor Standards Act of 1938* established minimum wage laws, overtime laws, and abolished child labor among other things. In a very real sense, by 1938 *organized labor* had won victories in its long struggles against injustices. The answers to all the legitimate concerns of organized labor were now accomplished.

The *civil rights* movement followed a similar pattern. The Thirteenth Amendment to end slavery was adopted in 1865. The Civil Rights Act of 1866 was passed to give "*Negroes*" citizenship and protect freed men from Black Codes and other repressive legislation. The First Reconstruction Act of 1867 gave the federal government more control over the solidly Democrat South. The Fourteenth Amendment in 1868 to make all persons born in the US citizens was intended specifically to protect Black former slaves. The Fifteenth Amendment in 1870 gave Black folks the right to vote. The *Anti Ku Klux Klan Act of 1871* was to give legal protection to Black people. The *Civil Rights Act of 1875* prohibited racial discrimination in public accommodations.

All these laws, including three constitutional amendments, were passed more than 130 years ago. All these laws were passed by

REPUBLICANS over the strenuous objections of the Democrat Party.

Republican controlled Congresses passed Civil Rights Acts in 1957 and 1960 both of which were signed by President Eisenhower, a REPUBLICAN. The U.S. Civil Rights Commission was established in 1958, again under REPUBLICANS during the Eisenhower administration. The *Civil Rights Act of 1964* was passed by a majority consisting of more REPUBLICANS than Democrats. Key Democrat Senators, including Al Gore, Sr. of Tennessee opposed it.

There has been no legally sanctioned discrimination on the basis of race in the United States in over forty years! In fact, by the early 1970's the pendulum swung the other way, and today, in many cases, Black folks actually have more legal rights and economic opportunities for advancement. It is now white folks discriminated against in employment, promotions, government contracts, and college admissions, all in the name of *affirmative action*. *Affirmative action* is a Politically Correct euphemism for racial discrimination against white people and Asians.

The *tea party* movement has not, at least so far, reached stage five. There have been no landmark legislative or judicial victories address the economic disasters that gave rise to the *tea party* movement. We have not reformed the tax code. We do not yet have a balanced budget amendment to the constitution, and so far, we have not been able to abolish a single wasteful or unconstitutional government agency.

The *tea party* movement did contribute to major election victories in the 2010 mid-term elections. One reason that has not led to hoped for legislative victories has to do with the Democrat Party still being in control of the White House and the U.S. Senate. Remember, it took the *labor* and *civil rights* movements between fifty and seventy-five years to achieve legislative victories. By that standard, the *tea party* is still in diapers, and its accomplishments in only three years have been remarkable.

SURVIVAL OF THE FAMOUS:

Stage six in the life cycle of a political or social movement is the survival of the famous, long after the crisis that generated the movement has been solved. Organized labor won all its legitimate goals seventy-three years ago. They have the legal right to organize unions. Today there is no child labor; the 40-hour week, overtime, and a minimum wage are all permanent parts of our legal system.

After 1938 there was no longer any real justification for the organized labor movement, they won great victories for the working classes. The industrial excesses of the 19th century were ended and there was no longer any great crisis to justify a national social movement among the working class. It would have been reasonable for organized labor to disband its formidable political machine, stop the strikes, end the violence, fire its armies of paid goons, run off the reds and their sympathizers, and finally live in peace with their neighbors in the community.

Why did this not happen? It did not happen because labor had moved into stage six in the life of a social movement. Stage six begins after the crisis is long over and the movement has been victorious and achieved all its legitimate goals. At that point you might predict the movement would throw a huge victory party and go home. You would be wrong.

Hundreds of the smaller organizations created to correct problems, mostly local in nature all won victories. Particularly in the case of organized labor, these hundreds of small organizations understood there is power in numbers. They formed alliances, coalitions, and in most cases, were simply gobbled up to become local chapters of much larger conglomerates of labor organizations.

Many small unions were consolidated into huge, powerful, mega unions like the American Federation of Labor (AFL). The AFL was one of the organizations able to promote the labor movement by organizing strong craft unions, each representing a particular trade or craft such as carpenters, machinists, electricians, plumbers, boilermakers, and so forth. The AFL stressed strong apprenticeship programs and kept out unskilled craftsmen.

In 1935 more militant unionists, most with strong communist ties, wanted to organize whole industries, not just particular crafts. This concept was called Industrial Organization. The advocates of Industrial Organization wanted to organize all workers in a particular industry, whether they were skilled craftsmen or not. They formed an organization, the Congress of Industrial Organizations (CIO) initially as a group within the AFL. The AFL responded by expelling the CIO unions. The CIO, under the leadership of John L. Lewis, continued to function for the next twenty years as a separate organization, till in 1955, the two factions re-united to form the AFL-CIO.

Unions did not die out after laws were passed guaranteeing health, safety, good wages, and elimination of child labor. The unions were now a multi-million dollar business that employed thousands of bureaucrats as if it was an arm of government. All these very well paid union employees were not about to declare victory and disband. Instead, they moved from defending the underdog against unfair practices, to extorting more wages and benefits than they would ever earn in a free market. They moved deeper and deeper into politics becoming, in effect, the GOTV arm of the Democrat Party.

In the 1920's, 30's, and 40's the unions often supported the Communist Party of the USA (CPUSA) or one of several other leftist and socialist parties. Many labor leaders in those years actually considered FDR and the Democrats to be too conservative! Many of the leaders and much of the labor funding came from the Soviet Union via the CPUSA and while Russia was in league with Hitler early in the war, these union leaders objected to FDR's support for the British.

The alliances between the far left, and the Democrat Party continue right up to this day. Only the Black population supported Barack Obama any stronger than organized labor. Obama repaid labor with billions in bailouts and insider deals that have left the United Auto Workers Union more or less in control of General Motors. Obama's massive stimulus plan was targeted almost exclusively to employees in the government sector of the economy, and to unions that supported Obama. The stimulus was never about creating jobs. It was always about giving almost a trillion dollars to the unions who put the Obama regime in power.

His current $435 Billion *"Jobs Bill"* is nothing more than additional payola to these same unions and their goons.

The civil rights movement followed a similar path. There have been hundreds of *civil rights* organizations over the last 125 years. As we have noted, in the beginning Black people had legitimate complaints and aspirations for improving themselves economically.

Herman Cain correctly points out, many of the Black folks in America have been brainwashed into supporting people and organizations that have not always, or even often, had their best interests at heart. The Black people in America have been victimized and oppressed at least as much by their self-proclaimed friends, as they ever have been by any white man.

Most rank and file Black people genuinely wanted to obtain the equal protection of the law and improve themselves economically. The plethora of organizations and self proclaimed leaders often just wanted to enrich themselves by loudly complaining about the "*plight of the poor Negro.*" Other organizations, including the national Democrat Party, have blatantly pushed every sort of socialist power grab, and every excuse for centralizing power in the federal government, all in the name of improving conditions for the "*poor Negro.*"

After fifty years of such help, the Black community has seen a rise in Black unemployment, an increase in births to Black unwed mothers, and continued Black-on-Black crime. Politicians, unions, bankers, the Democrat Party, the CPUSA, and a whole lot of self-appointed Black leaders, have seen the Black population as merely a pawn on a chessboard to be moved around or sacrificed in the game of obtaining money and power.

As with organized labor, hundreds of civil rights organizations have existed since the turn of the last century and have now been consolidated into a couple of dozen key organizations. Those remaining groups employ hundreds of thousands of people directly and control budgets in the billions of dollars. Civil rights laws long ago ended any legal discrimination against the Black people in America. However, these organizations are not about to declare victory and disband.

Those organizations and institutions grew out of the struggle to solve a problem, but survive long after the problem has been solved. The new mission of these institutions is now to continue to collect dues, make payroll, issue publications, host a website, and provide an upper class living for their leaders and key employees.

In the cases of *labor* and *civil rights*, they now cry wolf about problems, some of which were solved a century ago, in order to rake in more money today. There are now no Black people in America who are held in slavery, denied the right to vote by law, none who are required to ride on the back of the bus, none who are prohibited from serving on juries, none who are prohibited from entering a public restaurant, and none who are denied a job, a loan, or admission to a university because of the color of their skin. Most tea party supporters would gladly march in the streets beside the Rev. Al Sharpton if there were any.

PERPETUAL AGITATION:

The seventh stage in the development of political and social movements is to perpetually agitate for more power and influence. No organization that tells its dues paying members *we won, mission accomplished* can give them any reason to continue to pay dues. No organization with a web page proclaiming *we have accomplished all the goals related to our original mission statement* is ever going to be able to write a successful multi-million dollar grant request to a foundation. Admitting *we have nothing left to complain about* will never fill campaign coffers, or elect radicals to congress.

There must be a boogieman out there somewhere. When folks no longer try to offend you, take offense at something anyway. Organizations that once promoted safe working conditions and fair wages, now promote class warfare, and wealth redistribution.

People who once had little political power, now seek to consolidate total control, and achieve a strangle hold on the American economy. Organizations that once fought racial discrimination against Black people, now dream up justifications for demanding legislation that is nothing more than racial discrimination against white people. The movement has long since ceased to be about fundamental fairness or the rule of law. Now it is just about getting as much money and power as you can get - at the expense of other races.

In summary, the stages in the life of every political or social movement of lasting effect consist of, crisis, public protest of the crisis, multiple organizations are created to address the crisis, they generate sympathy for the victims, this leads to legislation to correct the problem and end the crisis.

These five stages are followed by survival of the prominent, and now powerful organizations long after the crisis was averted or the injustice corrected and finally massive permanent agitation and fund-raising in the name of a long gone crisis or injustice.

The *tea party* movement has gone through four of those seven stages in a remarkably short three years, compared to decades required by *labor* and *civil rights* organizations. Speculation about whether the *tea party* movement is a flash-in-the-pan, or becomes permanent will turn on its ability to enter stage five and succeed in enacting legislation to address the current cultural and economic crisis.

The tea party movement is demanding Cut, Cap & Balance to

solve the economic portion of our current crisis. The word balance refers to the need for a Balanced Budget amendment to the U.S. constitution. We have already noted there is a real need for currency reform as well as reform of our tax laws. Accomplishing these necessary reforms will require electing a majority of the U.S. Senate in 2012, retaining control of the U.S. House of Representatives and electing a Republican president.

Once the tea party movement gets past those hurdles, it will be necessary to insure those Republican majorities have the backbone to actually enact the necessary reforms. We do not just want lip service in the GOP platform; we want legislative enactments signed into law by the next Republican president. Passing a Balanced Budget Amendment does not require the signature of the President but must be approved by the legislatures of ¾ of the states (38 out of 50).

As this book goes to press, the most salient feature of the tea party movement is the total lack of organization, lack of structure, and the absence of any leaders of national stature who can speak for the whole of this very fluid phenomenon. There are no worries the tea party movement may some day follow labor and civil rights into stages six and seven where giant organizations with huge budgets survive to agitate about imaginary problems.

APPENDIX A

Conservative Organizations:

There are quite a few organizations today that are able to provide you with information, training, and the opportunity to connect with parts of the tea party movement in your community. I am not a member, officer, employee, etc., of any of these organizations. I do not have any connection with any of them, other than as a user of information or training and other services they provide. This list is certainly not complete, nor is it an exhaustive list of other similar organizations that also provide information and services.

I will update and expand this list from time to time. For my most up to date evaluation of the usefulness of the various conservative and tea party type organizations in our country, see my website at **www.RattlesnakeRevolution.com** which is regularly updated. The print version of Rattlesnake Revolution will be difficult to keep current because conservative, and particularly tea party type, organizations are constantly being created, joining forces to form alliances, splitting apart to form competing factions, and upon occasion, changing names over time. The latest information will always be on our website.

Instead, my goal is to list organizations that are useful to any reader of _Rattlesnake Revolution_ and to the leaders and members of local tea party and other conservative organizations. I have included many of the major conservative organizations in this guide because the wealth of information and resources they provide can be invaluable to tea party leaders seeking to increase their effectiveness and form alliances with large established organizations and political communities are your natural allies. The descriptions are taken from the organizations themselves.

Accuracy in Academia

4455 Connecticut Avenue, N. W.

Suite #330

Washington, DC 20008

academia.org

(202) 364-3085

Accuracy in Academia, a non-profit research group based in Washington, D. C., wants schools to return to their traditional mission-the quest for truth. To promote this goal, AIA documents and publicizes political bias in education in *Campus Report,* its monthly newsletter. CR articles focus on:

The use of classroom and/or university resources to indoctrinate students;

Discrimination against students, faculty or administrators based on political or academic beliefs; and

Campus violations of free speech.

Accuracy in Media [Founded 1969]

4455 Connecticut Avenue, N.W.
Suite #330
Washington, D.C. 20008
(202) 364-4401

Accuracy in Media is a citizens' media watchdog whose mission is to promote accuracy, fairness and balance in news reporting. AIM exposes politically motivated media bias; teaches consumers to think critically about their news sources; and holds the mainstream press accountable for its misreporting.

American Conservative Union [Founded 1964]

1007 Cameron Street

Alexandria, Virginia 22314

(703) 836-8602

Conservative.org

ACU represents the views of Americans who are concerned with economic growth through lower taxes and reduced government spending and the issues of liberty, personal responsibility, traditional values and national security.

CPAC – the Conservative Political Action Conference is the nation's largest gathering of conservatives annually. It is a project of ACUF and its largest annual conference.

American Enterprise Institute [Founded 1943]

1150 17th Street, N, W.

Washington, DC 20036

(202) 862-5800

aei.org

The American Enterprise Institute is a community of scholars and supporters committed to expanding liberty, increasing individual opportunity and strengthening free enterprise. AEI pursues these unchanging ideals through independent thinking, open debate, reasoned argument, facts and the highest standards of research and exposition. Without regard for politics or prevailing fashion, we dedicate our work to a more prosperous, safer and more democratic nation and world.

American Majority [Founded 2008]

P.O. Box 87
Purcellville, VA 20134
Phone: (540) 338-1251

American Majority is the leading developer of the nation's new 21st century grassroots political infrastructure. The organization uses its cutting edge training curriculum to empower individuals and organizations with the most effective tools to promote liberty through limited government. American Majority trains thousands of activists and candidates each year in communities across the country to be catalysts for authentic change in government. As of November, 2011, American Majority has conducted 544 trainings in 44 different states, training more than 19,000 candidates and activists (with most of work coming between April of 2009 and October of 2011).

Campaigns & Elections Magazine [Founded 1980]

1901 N. Moore Street
Suite 1105
Arlington, VA 22209
703-778-4028

campaignsandelections.com

Campaigns & Elections is the preeminent "how-to" journal of politics, focused on the tools, tactics and techniques of the political consulting profession.

Center For Immigration Studies [Founded 1985]

1522 K Street N.W., Suite 820
Washington, DC 20005-1202
Phone: (202) 466-8185

cis.org

The Center for Immigration Studies is an independent, non-partisan, non-profit, research organization. Since our founding in 1985, we have pursued a single mission – providing immigration policymakers, the academic community, news media, and concerned citizens with reliable information about the social, economic, environmental, security, and fiscal consequences of legal and illegal immigration into the United States.

Citizens Against Government Waste [Founded 1984]

1301 Pennsylvania Avenue, N.W.

Washington, DC 20004

(202) 467-5300

cagw.org

Citizens Against Government Waste (CAGW) is a private, non-partisan, non-profit organization representing more than one million members and supporters nationwide. CAGW's mission is to eliminate waste, mismanagement, and inefficiency in the federal government. Founded in 1984 by the late industrialist J. Peter Grace and syndicated columnist Jack Anderson, CAGW is the legacy of the President's Private Sector Survey on Cost Control, also known as the Grace Commission.

In 1982, President Reagan directed the Grace Commission to "work like tireless bloodhounds to root out government inefficiency and waste of tax dollars." For two years, 161 corporate executives and community leaders led an army of 2,000 volunteers on a waste hunt through the federal government. The search was funded entirely by voluntary contributions of $76 million from the private sector; it cost taxpayers nothing. The Grace Commission made 2,478 recommendations which, if implemented, would save $424.4 billion over three years, an average of $141.5 billion a year all without eliminating essential services.

Congressional Pig Book Summary is CAGW's famous exposé of the most glaring and irresponsible pork-barrel projects in the 13 annual appropriations bills and their sponsors.

Competitive Enterprise Institute [Founded 1984]

1899 L Street N.W. Floor 12

Washington, DC 20036

cei.org

Phone (202) 331-1010

Non-profit, public policy organization dedicated to advancing free enterprise and limited government.

The Conservative Caucus [Founded 1974]

450 Maple Avenue East

Vienna, Virginia 22180

(703) 938-9626

conservativeusa.org

Tea party before there was any tea party. Numerous tools for conservative activism.

Family Research Council [Founded 1981]

801 G Street N. W.

Washington, DC 20001

(202) 393-2100

frc.org

Advancing family, faith, & freedom in public policy.

Federation For American Immigration Reform [Founded 1979]

25 Massachusetts Avenue, N. W.

Washington, DC 20001

(202) 328-7004

fairus.org

Promoting a sane immigration policy.

Freedom Works

400 North Capitol Street, N. W.

Suite 765

Washington, DC 20001

(202) 783-3870

Freedomworks.org

They train conservative activists - very pro tea party movement.

Gun Owners of America [Founded 1975]

8001 Forbes Pl

Suite 102

Springfield, VA 22151

(703) 321-8585

gunowners.org

These are the most dedicated, pure, and effective defenders of the Second Amendment. This is what the NRA should be and is not!

The Heritage Foundation [Founded 1973]

214 Massachusetts Avenue, N. E.

Washington, DC 20002
(202) 546-4400

heritage.org

Largest and most effective organization promoting free enterprise, limited government, a strong national defense, and individual freedom.

Jews for the Preservation of Firearms Ownership [Founded 1989]

P. O. Box 270143

Hartford, WI 53027

(262) 673-9745

jpfo.org

Very strong defenders of the Second Amendment with lots of great material.

Leadership Institute [Founded 1979]

1101 North Highland Street

Arlington, Virginia 22201

(703) 247-2000

leadershipinstitute.org

"The Leadership Institute's mission is to increase the number and effectiveness or conservative activists and leaders in the public policy process." They have the best, oldest, and most effective, training programs for this purpose and are particularly influential with youth and on college campuses.

Minuteman Civil Defense Corps

Declaration Alliance

P.O. Box 1310

Herndon, Virginia 201727

minutemanhq.com

Minuteman Project [Founded 2005]

P. O. Box 3944

Laguna Hills, California 92654

(949) 587-5199

minutemanproject.com

A multi-ethnic immigration law enforcement advocacy group.

National Federation of Republican Women [Founded 1938]

124 N. Alfred Street

Alexandria, Virginia 22314

(703) 548-9688

nfrw.org

Very effective in training activists and working for the conservative ideals in the GOP platform.

National Right to Work Committee [Founded 1955]

8001 Braddock Road

Suite 500

Springfield, VA 22160

(800) 325-7892

nrtwc.org

Fights compulsory unionism.

National Tea Party Federation [Founded 2010]

info@thenationalteaparty.com

Tea Party Caucus [Founded 2010]

Michele Bachmann, Chairman

103 Cannon HOB

Washington, DC 20515

(202) 225-2331

http://bachmann.house.gov/TeaPartyCaucus/

Currently 66 members of Congress, including several members of the leadership as well as the Chairman of the Judiciary Committee have joined this influential and growing group within the US Congress to work for limited government and individual freedom. Urge your Representative to join.

Tea Party Express [Founded 2009]

infor@teapartyexpress.org

teapartyexpress.org

Very effective group has organized national bus tours to limit the size and intrusiveness of the federal government.

Tea Party Nation

teapartynation.com

Social network for the tea party movement.

Tea Party Patriots [Founded 2009]

teapartypatriots.org

Non-profit organization 501 (c)(4) to restore America's founding principles of fiscal responsibility, constitutionally limited government, and free markets.

Young Americans for Freedom [Founded 1960]

110 Eden Street

Herndon, Virginia 20170

(800) USA-1776

yaf.org

One of the most influential conservative organizations of the last fifty years. Alumni include Ronald Reagan, Dan Quayle, and numerous members of congress. On February 14, 2011 YAF expelled Congressman Ron Paul from its Advisory Board because of his "delusional" foreign policy and alliances with left wing anti-war organizations.

APPENDIX B

Tea Party Checklist

Whether you are creating an organization from scratch, or reorganizing an existing group to become more effective, there are a number of basic elements necessary for success. These elements include:

· Having a clear and well-defined purpose for the organization.

· Having a written Mission Statement expresses purpose succinctly.

· Selecting a distinct name reflects your mission.

· Adopting a set of written by-laws to govern your group effectively.

· Incorporating in your state.

· Obtaining a federal Tax I.D. number.

· Opening a bank account.

· Having dues paying members.

· Electing a board of officers to administer the organization.

· Have a professional website in the Internet.

· Have a Facebook page for your organization.

· Obtaining non-profit status from the IRS pursuant to IRC § 501 (c)(3).

· Hold regular officers meetings to plan activities.

· Hold regular membership meetings to carry out those plans.

· Have functioning standing committees for Fund Raising, Membership Recruiting, Budget & Planning, Public Relations, and Newsletter.

· Engage in community service projects.

· Engage in political action programs.

Hold training and seminars on how to be effective in the
political process.

APPENDIX C

Some pundits on the far left have tried to compare the tea party movement with the Occupy Wall Street demonstrations. Here is the comparison. I will let you decide for yourself if you believe there are any similarities.

Reported	Occupy Wall Street	Tea Party
Arrests	4149	0
Rapes	12	0
Damage	$10,000,000.00	$0.00
Public Defecation	Yes	No
Anti-Semitic Rants	12	0
Cost to Taxpayers (through 9/2011)	$19,327,487.00	$0.00
Public Masturbation Incidents	3	0
Molotov Cocktails Thrown	10	0
Fights Started	Yes	No
Children Exploited	Yes	No
Police Cars Damaged	2	0

Public Drunkenness	Yes	No
Drug Possession Arrests	Yes	No
Concealed Weapons Arrests	Yes	No
Drug Overdose	Yes	No
Thefts	Yes	No
Burglaries	Yes	No
Vandalism Arrests	Yes	No
Trespassing Arrests	Yes	No
Non-fatal Shootings	1	0
Public Urination	Yes	No
Urination On Others	Yes	No
Israeli Flags Burned	2	0
American Flags Burned	1	0
American Flags Danced On	1	0
American Flag Desecration	25	0
Felony Assault on an EMT	1	0
Head/Body Lice Outbreaks	1	0
Tuberculosis Outbreaks	1	0
Murder	1	0
Suicide	1	0
Shots Fired at White House	1	0
Scabies Outbreaks	1	0

Endorsements:	O.W.S.	Tea
Obama Endorsed	Yes	No
Pelosi Endorsed	Yes	No
CAIR Endorsed	Yes	No
Socialist Party Endorsed	Yes	No
Nazi Party Endorsed	Yes	No
Muslim Brotherhood Endorsed	Yes	No
Communist Party Endorsed	Yes	No
Biden Endorsed	Yes	No
Hugo Chavez Endorsed	Yes	No
Black Panthers Endorsed	Yes	No
Hezbollah Endorsed	Yes	No
Marxist Union Endorsed	Yes	No
9/11 Truther Endorsed	Yes	No
Bolshevik Endorsed	Yes	No
Iran Government Endorsed	Yes	No
Ayatollah Endorsed	Yes	No
North Korea Endorsed	Yes	No
Farrakhan Endorsed	Yes	No
Nation of Islam Endorsed	Yes	No

Thanks to Col. Ed Humphries, USAF (Retired) for researching this comparison.

Join the

Rattlesnake Revolution

Today!

Our website at www.RattlesnakeRevolution.com is a resource for all freedom loving Americans who are ready to take our country back. We are constantly adding additional materials and links to useful resources.

Selling **RATTLESNAKE REVOLUTION** is a great way to raise funds for your Tea Party organization or other group. Please contact us for quantity discounts. When your organization sells **RATTLESNAKE REVOLUTION** we automatically add your contact information and place a link to your website on ours.

RATTLESNAKE REVOLUTION is now being sold in a growing number of independent bookstores around the United States. If your bookstore purchases **RATTLESNAKE REVOLUTION** and carries it on your shelves, we will place your contact information on the website with a link to your website.

Dean Allen is available for radio and television interviews, book signings and other special events. Please tell us about any opportunities to promote **RATTLESNAKE REVOLUTION** in your area.

Dean Allen is available to teach an all day seminar on the nuts & bolts of politics for your organization.